I0008908

CODING INTERVIEW

A Beginner's Guide to Learn and Study the Theories
and Principles of Coding and Perform Well in the
Coding Interview

NOVA SYNTAX

© Copyright 2022 – All rights reserved.

The content contained within this book may not be reproduced, duplicated, or transmitted without direct written permission from the author or the publisher.

Under no circumstances will any blame or legal responsibility be held against the publisher, or author, for any damages, reparation, or monetary loss due to the information contained within this book, either directly or indirectly.

Legal Notice:

This book is copyright protected. It is only for personal use. You cannot amend, distribute, sell, use, quote or paraphrase any part, or the content within this book, without the consent of the author or publisher.

Disclaimer Notice:

Please note the information contained within this document is for educational and entertainment purposes only. All effort has been executed to present accurate, up to date, reliable, complete information. No warranties of any kind are declared or implied. Readers acknowledge that the author is not engaging in the rendering of legal, financial, medical, or professional advice. The content within this book has been derived from various sources. Please consult a licensed professional before attempting any techniques outlined in this book.

By reading this document, the reader agrees that under no circumstances is the author responsible for any losses, direct or indirect, that are incurred as a result of the use of information contained within this document, including, but not limited to, errors, omissions, or inaccuracies.

Table of Contents

Introduction

Coding interviews have changed over the years, and the expectations are now firmer than ever. Interviewers not only want to assess your programming skills but also want to assess your behavior during the interview. It is important to develop the right practices and attitude before you go for the interview. You need to display the right skills so the interviewer can hire you without a doubt. Your communication and problem-solving methods also give the interviewer a fair idea about how well you can approach different situations at work.

This book has all the information you need about coding interviews and leaves you with some example programs you can use in the interview. The book also has some tips and tricks you can use to determine how to behave in an interview. The list is not exhaustive, but it should give you an edge over the other applicants.

Go through the book and familiarize yourself with the information. Use the book as your guide before you begin working on the code. The book has all the information you need about coding and what you need to learn to ace the interview. You will not only learn about the different programming languages you can choose from but also how to choose the right language for the program you are trying to solve. The book also leaves you with some tips you can use to answer the interviewer and what you should keep in mind to leave a good impression on the interviewer.

Towards the end of the book, you will find a few common algorithms and programs interviewers want you to know. They will give you problems where you need to use these algorithms. If you master the use of these algorithms, you can solve any problem using decision, loop, and sorting/searching algorithms. Regardless of how amazing you are at coding, you need to practice if you want to ace the interview. Practice, practice, and more practice. That should be your motto.

Thank you for purchasing the book. I hope the information helps you do well during the interview. Good luck!

Chapter One

Coding Interview Prep

A coding interview is where the interviewer will assess both your technical and problem-solving skills. If you want to work in the field of coding, either as an engineer or data scientist, you must sit for a coding interview. During the interview, the interviewer will assess your knowledge of the system, architecture, design, algorithms, data structures, and more.

Most big tech companies have similar interview processes. While the processes may not be the same, it is important for you need to prepare yourself well to have the right skills before the interview.

You can speak to the interviewer before the actual interview date to understand the structure.

In a coding interview, the interviewer will ask numerous questions about different coding concepts. You will also be asked to solve a problem or two. To do this, you should write code in front of the interviewer.

During a coding interview, a company will evaluate your skills, especially your programming, technical and problem-solving skills. The interviewer will also assess your understanding of different programming concepts. The questions they ask you are dependent on the position. Throughout the interview, the interviewer will assess your abilities and skills and understand how well you solve a problem based on those skills.

Since coding interviews focus on problem-solving, the interview process is used to identify the people with the best skills. A part of the coding interview will also include behavioral questions, which are unrelated to how well you write code. Through a behavioral interview, the interviewer will try to assess if you can fit into the company and how well you handle different situations. It is also important for them to know how you present yourself in different social circumstances

Is It Okay to Change Programming Languages during the Interview?

Well, yes, you can do this. If you do choose to do this, let the interviewer know why you are changing the programming

4

language. Do not start writing the code using Java and switch to C++ because you think the latter is better to address the problem than the former. If you do want to make the switch, speak to the interviewer and let him know why you are making that decision. Let him know why the first choice was not the right one for the problem.

Moving to a different programming language because you are nervous or anxious lets the interviewer know you did not make a well-thought decision. You did not review the problem statement before you began writing the code. Before you write the code, you must determine the algorithm, so you can design the structure of the code. Speak to the interviewer and determine if he aligns with your process. He may give you some hints you can use to change the language.

If you want to write the code only in one language, it will not reflect negatively on you. Take some time to answer questions. Process the question, understand what you should do, and answer the interviewer confidently. In technical interviews, the interviewer focuses more on how you answer questions and approach a problem. He will not focus on how many programming languages you know.

It is also important to remember the different types of skills – primary and secondary. An interviewer would know this. You should avoid showing off in any interview. The objective is for you to prove you can accomplish a task.

What to Do after a Coding Interview

Before you finish the interview, you should ensure you have all the information you need about the next steps. Speak to the interviewer and ask him whom you should contact. You can also ask the interviewer if you want any feedback. It is also a good idea to send the interview a thank you note letting him know you are grateful for the time he spent on the interview. It is best to send the email to the interviewer within 48 hours of the interview.

It is also a good idea to reflect on how well you did in the interview. This is a good thing to do for your future interviews. Did you identify some concepts you should have gone over before the interview? You can also evaluate what you noted about the company. You can choose not to pursue the opportunity at the end of the interview. The role may not match your requirement. You can make this decision based on your assessment of the company.

Do I Need Specific Resources to Prepare?

It is not easy to crack a coding interview for obvious reasons. Preparing alone for the interview may make it difficult for you. You should practice as often as you can and learn from the people around you. You can also participate in different forums. Read various online forums and articles about coding interviews and do everything you can to improve.

Chapter Two

What to Do before, during, and after the Interview

When it comes to a coding interview or any interview for that matter, you will need some tips to avoid panicking. You need to keep a clear mind before, during, and after the interview. This chapter will look at some of the most popular and common tricks people use to remain calm.

Before the Interview

The day before your interview is when you will worry about your performance during the interview. You should sit down and find different tricks to ensure you maximize your performance. You will want a day when it is easy to write code without any bugs because your interviewer expects it. To do this, you should ensure your mind is in the zone. It is difficult to find the zone since few people

Get Some Sleep

You may want to study and cram as much as you can the night before the interview, but do not do this. You have to sleep. It is worse to interview when you are sleep deprived. It is better to get drunk and go for the interview. It should be your aim to sleep for at least 8 hours the night before your interview so you are calm and your brain has all the energy it needs. It may also be better to get some sleep for two days before the interview if you want your body to be active.

When the sun goes down, grab an early dinner and stop practicing. Do your best to relax. If you cannot sleep because of nervousness or pent-up energy, try one of the following:

- Do not drink any coffee in the afternoon
- Avoid alcohol for a few days before the interview
- Exercise during the day. Do not go all out, but take a walk or do some light exercise
- Do not stay online on your phone for a long time after the sun sets

- Consume a light dinner. You will not sleep properly if you feel too heavy. It is probably a good idea to eat brain-healthy food, such as beans, vegetables, and salmon

- Listen to music, a boring podcast, or read a book before you go to bed

Do not practice new problems before you go to bed. This will only make you anxious. Instead of doing this, you can choose to practice the problems you know best.

Practice the Things You Are Good At

If you want to be confident for your interview, practice those questions you know you can solve. You can work on difficult problems during the day but stop working on them before the evening. You need to focus only on what you know best. Only when you give yourself these small wins can you can remain confident for your interview. For example, if you are good at data structures, you can work on those problems for a few hours before bed. You will then dream only about data structures and problems you can solve, which will boost your self-esteem.

Visualize the Best Outcome

Focus on the best outcome before you go to bed. This tip is a positive reinforcement exercise, and it can sound weird. It is, however, something most entrepreneurs and athletes do before important interviews and games. You can also do guided meditation to know exactly how you should visualize the outcome.

If you do not think a guided meditation exercise is something you want to do, you can do something simple. Take a piece of paper and write down everything you want to happen so your day goes well. The following are some points you can include:

- Focus on your first interaction with the interviewers. Think of some small talk and see if you can sneak some jokes in

- They asked you the first question, and you crushed it. The interviewers are impressed with your answer

- You have now answered all the easy questions the interviewer has asked you. He will now move on to tougher questions. If you are unsure of the question, you should ask the interviewer to clarify. This is the only way for you to answer the question correctly

- In the final interview, you will speak to the director, and this conversation goes as well as expected. Your interview is finally done, and you can go home with the biggest smile on your face

Visualizing a positive outcome will make you confident about the interview. Doing this allows you to train your brain to focus on the positives and highs of the day. You will feel more confident and taste success.

List Down Your Process

It is imperative for you to focus on your problem-solving process. When you practice your problem-solving process, it reinforces the patterns or so we think. It is best to do this, especially before your interview. Consider the following tips:

1. Think about an algorithm. Consider a certain problem and focus on what the inputs and outputs would be. Think about these inputs aloud and see how you can gather this information. Do not start writing your code until both you and your interviewer feel particularly good about the algorithm you have selected

2. Once you have the algorithm in place, you should think about how we would want to structure the cold. You should focus on writing the code and add comments to each line or

section, so you will know if you should double-check anything later

3. Test your code. You should text the code using a simple input and see if it runs into any errors

It is best to focus on your problem-solving process on the day of the interview.

Prepare for Your Morning

It is difficult to make decisions on a whim. It is for this reason some people such as Barack Obama and Mark Zuckerberg choose to wear the same clothes. This will minimize the number of decisions they have to make every day. This is called decision fatigue. If you are aware of this fatigue, you can avoid it by planning your morning in advance. Consider the following:

- Pack the bag you are going to carry for the interview. You can include a notepad, water bottle, and a snack

- Decide what you want to wear. It is best to wear something a little more formal during an interview. Most people choose to work in a comfortable T-shirt or jeans. Do not make this mistake. Dress your best when you go for your interview

- Plan what you want to eat the following morning. It is a good idea to include berries, avocado, and eggs

- Decide the route you are going to take to get to the interview. Expect there to be traffic and plan for it. If you are driving to the office, figure out where you can park your car before you head in for the interview

- You should also decide when you need to wake up so you make it to the interview on time

- If you are someone who cannot wake up on time, you should set up more than one alarm so you wake up earlier than usual

- Think of a few things that will help you feel more energetic and active in the morning. You can think of a small workout, listen to good music, or even run for 20 minutes

Give Yourself an Energy Boost

Go for the interview with a positive mindset. Choose a routine with which you are comfortable. Such routines will help you feel confident and excited. You should feel great about your interview after your morning routine. The following are some activities you can include:

- Move your body. You can do a few jumping jacks, squats, or even sun salutations. It is best to stick to light exercise just to clear your mind

- Focus on positive affirmations and visualizations. This may seem a little strange in the beginning, but it does work. When you focus on the positive, you will feel confident before you head into the interview

- Listen to music to pump you up

During the Interview

You have now made it to your interview on time. So, what should you do during the interview?

Self-Introduction

It is important for you to begin your interview with a good self-introduction. It is best to restrict the amount of time you spend introducing yourself. If you spend too much time introducing yourself, you will not have enough time to complete and test your code. You should also sound enthusiastic, speak with this file and find ways to be more engaging.

Get Clarity

When the interviewer poses the question, it is a good idea to clarify it so you have understood it correctly. Never begin coding without getting clarity. Coding questions are often vague since interviewers want to understand how you think. Therefore, you should at least ask the interviewer three questions before you begin designing the algorithm. The following are some ways you can do this:

- Repeat the question to confirm you have understood the objective

- If you want to make any assumptions, clarify them before you begin your coding

- Understand the range the input values can take and determine the format in which the input values should be entered into the system

14

- Give the interviewer a simple example synonymous with the question posed

It is extremely important to understand what the interviewer is expecting and get the go-ahead from him before you begin coding.

Optimize the Approach

Work with the interviewer and identify a method best suited for you and optimize your effort. One of the biggest mistakes most people make during a coding interview is to dive directly into writing the code. This is a terrible idea because interviewers want you to discuss your approach with them, so they can understand how you think. They also want to see how well you work with others and whether you can bounce off ideas with another person before you begin writing the code. The conversation you have with them can last for either 5 or 10 minutes, depending on the complexity of the coding questions. During this time, you should gather hints from the interviewer, so you know the solution you have in mind is what the interviewer expects.

Write Your Code

Another way to ensure you have the right approach is to walk through the approach with the interviewer. As mentioned earlier, you should start coding only when the interviewer has given you the go-ahead. You need to explain your objective and why you write the code, too. You can also compare different approaches to determine whether you have the right one in mind. This will give you a chance to let the interviewer know how well you understand different programming languages.

Do not start writing your code at a fast pace. Write code at a pace which allows you to communicate with the interviewer and let him know your approach to the problem. Do Not spend too much time talking or explaining the code since you will have the time left to finish writing and testing your code.

It is also a good idea to avoid writing similar code. Write a working code, which you can compile at the end of the interview. It is also best to write neat, clean, and straightforward code. Try to minimize or reduce syntax errors. You should consider adopting good coding practices as per the language requirements.

When you write the code, avoid using complicated variable names. Let every variable being used in the code explain its function in the code. For example, if you write the program to sort ten elements in an array, you can name the function *sortingtenelements*. If you are unsure of whether the interviewer is OK with using a trivial function, you can confirm the same with him. Any assumptions or shortcuts you take should be mentioned in your code in the form of comments. Alternatively, you can also let the interviewer, so he understands your thought process

It is important to ensure you let your interviewer finish a sentence before you begin speaking to him. Bear in mind that your interviewer is only speaking to give you hints. While comments are an important factor to consider when writing code, you should not spend too much time doing the same during an interview. Avoid repeating yourself. Do not copy code without checking if it will work in the section of your code where you want to add it.

Test Your Code

When you have finished writing your code, you should review the code, check the comments, and run test cases. Never announce to the interviewer that you are done, even if you are done before time, unless you perform these steps. You should add test cases to the court so that you can improve on the existing code.

The first thing for you to do is read the entire code and look for any mistakes. You should think of the code as having been written by somebody else and review it with a critical eye.

Leave a Good Impression

It is important to leave the interview on a good note. Ask right that are related to the job and company. We will look at some questions you can consider later in the book. Never end any interview without asking the interviewer at least one question.

Ask the Right Questions

Once you finish the interview, you can ask the interviewer any questions you may have about the company or role. This is a great time for you to learn more about the company. The following are some questions you can ask:

- What is the best part about your job?
- What is the culture of the company?
- Can you choose the project you want to work on?
- What projects do you usually give to new joiners?

After the Interview

There are a lot of opportunities you may have during this time, but some people do find themselves in a difficult spot. For example, some people do not know when to connect with the interviewer or how they should approach them. In this section, we will look at some tips you can consider if you are worried about what you should do after the interview.

Ask for More Information

Getting all the necessary information from the interviewer before you leave the room is important. Ask the interviewer whom you should connect with for the next steps and when to expect a response from the team. This would give you an idea of how long the potential employer would take to give you the result. Instead of asking them for the next steps, you can ask them if there will be another interview or how many days they will take to get back to you.

Assess Your Performance

It may or may not be a good idea to assess your performance depending on whether it will affect you. If you want to assess your performance, you can write down all the questions asked during the interview and recall your answers. It is also important for you to include those points you wanted to say but did not. The objective is for you to see if a part of the interview did not go as well as expected and what you could have done. This assessment will help in the future.

Note Down What to Remember

If there is something specific you want to remember about the interview, you can note this information down, too. You do not have to remember all your answers, but if there is something specific you would want them to remember, you should record it. If you spoke to more than one person in the interview, write their names and designations down. Write down your thoughts about the office and whether you liked being in the environment. This information will help you if you have a second interview with a potential employer.

Be Grateful

It is important to thank the hiring manager or the interviewer within 24 hours of your interview. You should be grateful to them for taking the time to conduct the interview. If you do choose to write an email to the interviewer, you can add some notes or links about the industry. For instance, if you discuss a specific type of programming language, find some links for why it is true. You can send the details to the interviewer, so he knows where you are coming from. Alternatively, you can send a link to a forum you follow where experts in the field discuss numerous technical issues.

Connect with the Interviewer on Social Media

If you are on LinkedIn or other business networking social sites, you should see if the interviewer is there and connect with him. If they accept, then it could mean they want to learn more about you. This is one of the easiest ways to expand your professional network. You may end up in a different company or position in the same company, but this should not deter you from expanding your network.

Send Supporting Information

If you have any supporting documents you want to share with the interviewer, make sure to send them after the interview. It could be a written assessment, an essay, or even some consent forms. You should get back to them on priority about these.

Speak to Your References

Most employers ask for references; if the interviewer asks for yours, you should connect with the references after the interview. Let them know someone from the firm may contact them before submitting them as a reference. If you think they will be called, you should notify them. This way, they will know what to expect and from whom to expect the call.

Be Patient

You cannot expect the interviewer or potential employer to quickly get back to you. Spend the time after the interview assessing your interview, learning new skills, and preparing for the next interview. If you know some people within the company, you can ask them to check with the hiring manager about the status. You can also connect with them if you want more information about how you did. Do not worry but remain calm. Never call the hiring manager whenever you feel like but wait for them to get back to you in their own time. If they say you should expect some information in a week, then check with them after a week.

Chapter Three

Preparing for Behavioral Interviews

A behavioral interview is one of the most popular techniques employers use to assess potential employees. This interview focuses on a potential candidate's past behavior. For instance, they may not ask you a hypothetical question, such as "Tell me how you would approach a stressful situation at work." They may instead ask you the following, "Tell me about a time at work where you were under a lot of stress and how you coped with it."

In this chapter, we will look at some points to focus on when it comes to behavioral interviews.

- Review the job description and understand what the responsibilities are for the role
- List down your achievements, how you supported the team and met objectives on some important projects in your career
- Look at your performance in previous interviewers and assess what you could have done better
- Note down your achievements in your career
- Use the STAR method (explained later in the book) to structure your answers
- Answer questions honestly
- Record your responses or ask your friend to hear you out
- Do not speak for longer than two minutes when answering a question

With behavioral interview questions, an interviewer is trying to understand the following about you:

1. How did you conduct yourself in a real-world situation? Did you behave the way a manager should?

2. Did you add value to the situation? Did your actions help the team?

3. How you define different concepts, such as pressure and stress at work. Most people have different definitions for this, so they would want to understand what your threshold is

If you want to succeed in a behavioral interview, you need to be prepared. No answer is wrong, but the interviewer will understand who you are as a person. The questions asked are aimed at helping them understand who you really are. Honesty is indeed the best policy in these interviews. As mentioned earlier, practice and record your responses, so you can correct yourself if necessary

The STAR Method
Using the STAR method, you can structure any answer, especially behavioral interview questions. You can create a story with a premise that your interviewer can understand easily.

Situation
The situation helps you establish how you, as the protagonist in the story, responded, and it is a very important part of the story. So, the first thing you need to do is set the context. When you are setting the situation, you will tell the listener where and when the event occurred. For example, "The team was working on a nine-month engagement with one of the largest FMCGs in the world when the stakeholders decided to change the user story, which meant the code we had written was no longer relevant."

Task

Give the listener an overview of what you did in this situation. You could say, "My role as a team lead required me to work with the team and communicate with the client about the new changes. I also had to work with the team to determine if there was any part of the old code we could use."

Action

Now, let the listener know what you did. Say, "I implemented daily stand-ups and scrum calls with the team. I also had weekly meetings with the stakeholders to update them on where we were in terms of development. This made it easier for the team to know what to expect each week from the stakeholder. I also implemented checkpoints when we would release an iterative product to the stakeholders, so they could review and let us know if any changes were to be made. I also spoke to every team member, so I knew how they were handling the change and to determine if we could meet our deadlines."

Result

Finally, tell the interviewer how your actions helped and what the result was. For example, "The above approach helped us meet the deadline and deliver the product as per the requirements. It was incredibly rewarding for the entire team to succeed and do well under pressure."

Preparing for the Interview

Before you begin working on your responses to different questions, you should read the description carefully. Make sure you have the necessary qualifications and experience. Now, focus on each area in the description and think of a story for each area. Use the STAR technique we talked about above to write the story down. Ensure you clearly define the situation, task, action, and result.

Practice your responses aloud numerous times. You can either do this yourself or with a friend. Your answers should not be longer than two minutes. This means the answer must be concise.

If you fidget or stutter often, you must practice your responses since these are signs of low confidence. You must be comfortable with what you are telling the interviewer. While it is impossible to anticipate all behavioral questions, it is best to have situational stories for different types of questions. This will give you the confidence you need to answer any question.

Examples of Behavioral Questions

The following section includes common behavioral questions the interviewer may ask. Spend some time on each question and prepare a sample answer for each of these. Prepare and plan for your interviews in advance.

- When you found yourself facing a problem at work, how did you handle it?

- If you have made a mistake at work, how did you address it? Did you own up to it and handle it well?

- What steps did you and your team take to overcome challenges at work?

- What new skills did you learn at work? How did you use it in your projects?

- How did you pitch an important idea to your seniors or stakeholders? Did they approve it?

- What strategies do you use to handle conflicts at work?

- Were there situations at work you think you could have handled differently?

- How did you overcome stressful situations at work?

- How did you achieve a goal you set for yourself?

- What about your work are you most proud of?

Chapter Four

How to Introduce Yourself

Your self-introduction is an important aspect to consider because this has an impact on your interview. You will introduce yourself to many people in the organization you are interviewing for. You should consider the following aspects when you introduce yourself in any interview.

Before the Interview

Before you sit with the interviewer or hiring manager, you need to introduce yourself to the HR or receptionist when you enter the building. When you do this, you should give the person your full name and let them know why you are visiting the office. You should also mention the role for which you are interviewing.

You can smile and shake hands. Ensure your grip is firm and you are polite. Do not crush the other person's hand, but only give it a firm shake. You can introduce yourself in the following manner: "Hi, I am John, and I am here to interview for the role of lead programmer. My interview is scheduled for 12 PM."

If the person introduces themselves to you, you can use the following to respond to them: "Hi <Name of the person>, it is nice to meet you. I hope you are having a good day." When you do this, you show them respect. This statement will cement you in their minds, and the person may react to you positively.

Now, you may be asked to wait for the hiring manager or interviewer to call you into the meeting room. Regardless of what the person tells you, thank them for the information.

Introducing Yourself in the Interview

While you wait for the interview to begin, drink some water. Find a way to calm yourself down. Speak to the other people around you. Get your book and pen out if you do not want to talk to others. Try mindfulness and visualization exercises while you wait. In some companies, you may have more than one interview on the same day. During these interviews, the interviewers will assess different abilities and skills you have. So, tailor your introduction and answers based on the interview.

When the interviewer approaches you, sit up straight and make eye contact. If they call for you, walk towards them with a confident stride and extend your hand. Now, give them a brief smile and shake hands with a firm grip. You can introduce yourself in the following way: "Good morning. It is a pleasure to meet you. Thank you for taking the time out."

After you exchange formalities, give them your documentation and wait. Do not begin the conversation. Wait for the interviewer to start.

What Should You Say to the Hiring Manager?
The hiring manager can be anybody in the team you are applying to. This individual will determine whether you will join the organization or not. This means the hiring manager has a lot of influence on the outcome of your interview. Therefore, you have to ensure your self-introduction is to the point. Ensure you cover all points in your self-introduction if you believe it will impact your interviewer's impression of you. If you thought about body language, you thought right.

You have to exude confidence when you introduce yourself. Do not panic if you stutter. You may be nervous, and this is bound to happen. Excuse yourself for a minute if you do stutter, collect your bearings, and continue. You need to be professional during the interview.

Once you finish exchanging pleasantries with the interviewer, he is going to ask you to introduce yourself. Keep the above in mind and talk about the role and how your skills and capabilities will help you in the role. Let the interviewer know how you think you can contribute to the firm. It is important to keep the introduction down to 2 minutes.

You can go to your elevator pitch if the interviewer asks for more information. Use adjectives that best describe you as an employee. Any word you use should only leave a positive impact on the interviewer. Avoid reading from a help card and keep the conversation natural.

What Should You Do after the Interview?

As H.W. Longfellow said, "Great is the art of beginning, but greater is the art of ending."

Let me give you a scenario. John introduced himself well when he was practicing his self-introduction before the interview. On the day of the interview, he gave everybody a great self-introduction. He did not do too well during the technical round, but he did make notes about the mistakes he made during the interview. He made a note of what he could do better the next time. When the interview came to an end, he thanked the interviewer for his time and smiled at him before he left the room. A few days later, he received a call from the organization for a follow-up interview. Since he made notes about where he would improve, he did well in the next round and secured the job.

Do you think the interviewer would have called him back if John did not end the interview on the right note? John knew he had to end the day amicably even if the interview went terribly. You should do this, too.

Tips and Tricks

You now have a brief idea about how you should introduce yourself in the interview. Let's now focus on your delivery. This section has some tips and tricks you can use to ace the introduction.

Never Be Late

You cannot prove you are serious about a role if you reach the interview late. Do not make people wait for you. To create a good first impression, you should be punctual. Keep this in mind in any professional situation. This will let the interviewer know you are serious about your application.

If you are being called to the office for the interview, reach the office the minute it opens. This way, you will understand the work culture and how the teams function daily.

Research

When it comes to an interview, you should research the interviewer, the company, and its culture. You can also look at the experience others have had when they interviewed with the organization. Understand what the job description means and tailor your conversation and introduction to the skills and responsibilities mentioned in the description.

Prepare relevant points you can use as conversation starters. When you ask the interviewer questions, you should include these points. Speak to the interviewer if you have questions about the culture or anything to do with the role. How well you prepare will determine the impression you create on the interviewer.

The interviewer can also assess how you would prepare for work based on your preparation for the interview. Preparing the interview will also help you remain calm and collected when you answer any questions the interviewer may ask you.

Assess the Room

If you reach the office early, you should use the time to read the room. See how the people in the office talk to each other. Is everybody calm in the office? Are they worried about something? Read the room. You can also assess the power dynamics in the office by looking at everybody around you. Using your assessment, try to change your introduction and focus on how you would answer the questions.

Dress Well

It is important to wear the correct dress depending on the occasion. You can form a first impression of the interviewer and everybody around you in a few seconds. This impression is dependent on your physical appearance and attire. If you walk into the interview with a crumpled shirt or unkempt hair, the interviewer is not going to be impressed. This will make him believe you are not serious about the interview.

Spend some time on your clothing and dress appropriately. Polish your shoes and ensure your clothes are not wrinkled. This will show you have covered the basics and are focused on your interview. In case you wear a new outfit, you should try it the day before the interview. This way, you can choose a backup outfit if needed and always wear comfortable and smart formal clothes.

Maintain Eye Contact

You should minimize your distractions and focus on the people around you. How would you feel when the person you speak to looks everywhere except you? You would feel ignored. This means you should also avoid behaving this way. When you ask or answer questions, pay attention to the interviewer. Maintain eye contact as often as possible. If you keep looking away, you may seem disinterested in the conversation, and this is not an impression you want to make. Focus on the person in front of you.

Watch Your Body Language

As mentioned earlier, nonverbal communication is important. It is more important than your self-introduction. If you want to come across as a confident or dependable person, you should avoid being nervous. Hold your chin high and sit straight. Take deep breaths if you are nervous.

Either the person you speak to when you enter the office or the interviewer will assess your confidence based on how firm your handshake is. Your eye contact also determines whether the person you talk to is impressed with you or not. If you do not know how your body language can come off during an interview, ask someone to watch you when you practice so that they can tell you about your strengths and weaknesses.

Give a Brief Professional Introduction

Your introduction should be engaged, concise, and to the point. The interviewer should be intrigued by what you say. If you want to capture the interviewer's attention, do the following:

- Show the interviewer how interested you are in the role

- Begin the conversation with a smile

- Talk about your professional experience and your achievements

- Highlight your skills based on the job description

You can also give the interviewer some facts about your personal life if you want to build a rapport with him. You can include information about the city you are from, what you studied in college, and why.

Practice

You need to practice your self-introduction before the interview. Keep practicing it if you have to. This goes for any prep you are doing. It is important for you to do this, especially when it comes to your interview. You should add this to the list of things you should do before the interview.

In addition to the behavioral, coding, and technical questions, you need to prepare your self-introduction. Write down an introductory statement and practice until you are certain you can deliver it without stuttering.

List Down Follow-up Questions

The interviewer may have some questions based on what you tell him. Identify those questions and think of how you would answer them. You may have mastered your behavioral and technical questions but think of some questions the interviewer may ask about your self-introduction.

The objective behind doing this is to increase your confidence. If you know you can answer any follow-up question, you will be sure about yourself. This will show up in your body language and in your manner of speaking with the interviewer. You need to learn to maintain your composure even when you do not feel too great about a question.

Chapter Five

Programming Languages

Numerous programming languages are being developed these days, and most of these new languages are all-purpose and general languages. Having said that, every programming language has its own pros and cons, so you need to choose the one you can learn easily. It is best to choose a mainstream programming language so the interviewer knows you are learning the popular languages, too.

You can classify programming languages into numerous categories, but each of these languages supports different programming styles. Numerous programming languages are being developed every year, but only some have gained popularity since programmers find it easy to use these languages.

Most programmers use programming languages to control or improve the performance of a computer. Since you can choose from numerous languages, it is important for you to understand the differences between these languages. This understanding will make it easier for you to choose the right language. This chapter sheds some light on the different types of programming languages and talks about the differences between the languages.

What Is Programming Language?

Machines or computers perform certain functions depending on the instructions you give them. These instructions can only be given using programming languages, which are a type of notation that computers understand. You can use these languages to control the activities machines perform. Developers have produced more than a thousand programming languages, but only some of them are very popular. You must choose the programming language depending on what activity you want the machine to perform. Every programming language is defined based on certain regulations and standards.

This chapter covers the different programming languages and sheds some light on the differences between the languages. Numerous other languages, such as Python, Prolog, C#, COBOL, and

Smalltalk, are like the abovementioned ones. You need to identify the language suitable for the question or problem the interviewer has given you.

Types of Programming Languages

Now that you have an idea about what a programming language is, let us look at programming language types.

Procedural Programming Language

If you want to execute a set of instructions, either in a sequence or not, use a procedural programming language. In this type of language, you can use different data structures, conditional statements, loops, variables and others. Using procedural programming languages, you can control how variables work, and control the value returned by the variable through any function.

Functional Programming Language

Functional programming languages depend on the information or data stored temporarily in the system. Such languages allow the use of recursive functions, and it is best to avoid using loops. The objective of these languages is to only return the output from functions

Logic Programming Language

Logic programming languages always allow the developer or programmer to make declarative statements. These languages then allow the machine to understand the consequences of each of those declarative statements. If you write a program using this language, you do not have to instruct the computer how to perform the activity. You will only employ some restrictions on how it should think. This is like unsupervised machine learning that we covered earlier in the book.

Different Programming Languages

C++ Language

The C++ language is an object-oriented programming language and is one of the most popular languages used by programmers to build large applications. A programmer can break a complex program into smaller sections making it easier for them to work on smaller programs. Since this is an object-oriented programming language, you can use one block of code multiple times. Some say this language is efficient, but others may not agree.

C Language

The C language is one of the most popular programming languages, and it is easy for anybody to understand. Most programmers prefer to use this language since the programs written run faster since the C language includes some additional features from C++. This language is used only because it also allows people to use some features from C++.

Pascal Language

If you are a beginner, you can learn this language. The Pascal language is often taught to students in school, and very few industries use this language to write code. If you are applying to an organization that uses this language, it will be good to understand how it works. Unlike most languages, this language does not use braces and symbols but uses keywords instead. This is why beginners learn this language very quickly.

Fortran Language

Fortran is the only programming language scientist's use. Storing variables of different lengths and sizes becomes easier using this language. Engineers or data scientists use this language to calculate precision values using Fortran. It is difficult to write code using this language though it may be difficult for a reader to understand the underlying calculations in your code. So, if you are applying for a data scientist or analyst position, you can look at some characteristics of this language and how you can use it.

Java Language

Java is a multi-platform language often used in networking. Most web applications use Java, and developers use this language to design web pages. Since this language has a format and syntax such as C++, developers can use this language to develop applications on cross platforms. Java is an extremely easy language for a C++ programmer to learn. Java is also an object-oriented programming language that makes it easier to develop numerous applications. It is slightly difficult to write code efficiently in Java, but the speed of the language has increased, and the latest version includes some features using which you can write programs easily. This is a language you can consider writing code in if you know how to use it.

Perl Language

The Perl language is used in systems compatible with the Unix operating system. Most often, developers use it to manage files on the operating system. If you are interviewing for a role where you should work with and manage the operating system, it is important for you to know this language.

This language is more popular for its CGI or Common Gateway Interface programming. Programmers use this language to look for text and to monitor databases and server functions. It is quite easy to learn the fundamentals of the language. Since Perl is used for CGI, many web developers prefer using this language over C++ to write code. Most website hosts or domains can read Perl scripts easily.

PHP Language

Since PHP is often used as a scripting language, developers often use this language to design applications and websites. The language has some features you can use to develop websites easily. Using these features, you can create a database for the website and generate different headers. These components also permit the developer to use some object-oriented features. It is for this reason most web developers use this language to develop a website.

LISP Language

LISP is a very common programming language used, and it stores different data structures, such as lists and arrays. It is easy to understand the code in this language since the syntaxes are easy for a beginner to understand. It is for this reason most people prefer to develop applications in this language.

Scheme Language

An alternative to the LISP language is the Scheme Language. That said, this language has simpler features and simpler syntax. When you work on building a project using the Scheme language, you will often re-implement the LISP language. This language is very introductory since it is easy to use. This language is also used to solve simple problems instead of worrying about the language's various syntaxes.

How Do You Choose the Type of Programming Language?

When it comes to a coding interview, the technical questions are asked to assess how well you approach a problem. This is when you also choose the programming language you want to write the code in. Before you choose the programming language, you should consider the following:

Introduction

This is the beginning of the interview, and it can last between three and five minutes. During this phase, the interviewer will try to learn more about you, your projects, and your background. It is during this moment you have to present yourself. This is your moment to shine and leave a good impression on the interviewer. Do not ignore this step. It is during this time you can try to assess exactly what the interviewer is looking for.

Be honest about who you are and talk about your work. Speak more about how you achieved something and why it was important for you to achieve it. The interviewer is constantly looking for a way to determine how well you approach problems, so talk about coding projects and how you achieved the objective.

Understand

When the interviewer poses a question, assess the question first. Understand it. The interviewer will give you the problem once you are ready. The problem is going to be concise and vague. It will include many details about corner cases, constraints, assumptions you can make, etc. This is when you should ask the interviewer anything you should know to clarify the question. Some questions you can ask include:

- What is the size of the input?
- Can the input take different values? What is the range it can take?
- Can you use duplicates in your code?
- Are there some extreme cases you should consider?

Search

Once you understand the problem fully, you focus on identifying the optimal solution. This is where your practice will come into play. You can determine what algorithm or data structure you can use to identify the solution. Most questions you practice before the interview will be like the ones the interviewer asks you. This means you will know what algorithm to use and which programming language to write the code in.

Write the Code

Once you determine the solution to the problem, you should start writing the code. If you want to write code you can compile easily without any bugs, you should know the language you choose. Some companies may ask you to write the code on a laptop/desktop or on a whiteboard. Therefore, you must remember the syntaxes in the language, so you write clean code. This will help the interviewer assess your knowledge of the language and read the code to understand your thought process. You can use comments to explain every line in the code. The interviewer may also ask you to fix a bug in your code.

Best Language to Use for an Interview

No language is the best language to use. The objective is for you to use the language with which you are comfortable. Some companies may give you a list of languages they would like for you to use, so you should select the language from there. If you apply for an entry-level job, choose a mainstream language. The company will teach you on the job.

You can choose a specific programming language if you want to do better than others and set yourself apart from them. Understand the company's technology and use the language they often use.

Tips for Writing a Program

You must consider the following principles when you write code, so you write clean code. You can give the interviewer three or more of the following principles, along with some examples for each of them.

Logging

When you write code, it will not compile or function the way you need it to since there are bound to be some bugs or errors in the code. Therefore, you must check the code for any errors by debugging it. It is important for you to do this even if you write code during the interview. Long programs will take you some time to review. In such situations, break the code into smaller segments and run the tests.

At the end of every test, you should create a log to store all the necessary information. Maintaining a log makes it easier for you to identify where the errors were in the code. You should always maintain a log of all the errors you find in your code, so you know exactly what to do when you debug.

Understand File Structure

It is essential for you to maintain structure in the code. It will be easier for you to understand and explain the code to the interviewer when you stick to the structure. The structure will vary based on the objective of the program. The idea will, however, remain the same.

Focus on Naming Conventions

You must stick to naming conventions when you write code. Name the methods, functions, variables, data structures and other elements in the code correctly to reduce errors.

If another person is checking your code, the names of the elements in your code should tell him what the elements are being used for. It is best to name variables based on their functionality and domain. Use the keyword 'is' if you have Boolean operators in your code.

If you want to develop a program or application for a bank to handle any payments made, consider using the following variables:

```
double totalBalance;          // Represents
the user account balance

double amountToDebit;         // Represents the
amount to charge the user

double amountToCredit;        // Represents the
amount to give to the user

boolean isUserActive;
```

Stick to the following naming conventions:

You must consider the following naming conventions and stick to them to maintain the code. Use the camel case when you label any variable or data structure.

For example,

```
int  integerArray[] = new int[10];
```

```
String   merchantName = "Perry Mason";
```

Using the screaming snake case to label constants. For example,

```
final long int ACCOUNT_NUMBER = 123456;
```

Indentation

If you want to use abstract classes or write some lines outside of a method, you are trying to create nests in the code. If you are trying to read another person's code, it will be difficult for you to determine when a specific module begins and ends. This happens because the person writing the code did not use indentation. Therefore, stick to indentation. You must let the reader know when a module begins or ends.

Learn to Assess Methods and Functions

If you use the right methods and functions in your code, you will be an expert at programming. Stick to the following rules when you name functions:

- Use camel case to name a function or method

- You must keep the method name on the same line as where you begin the method using the parentheses

- Name functions using a non-verb sound

- Ensure the functions only use one or two arguments. Debugging the code becomes difficult if you add too many arguments

For example,

```
double getUserBalance(long int
accountNumber) {

// Method Definition

}
```

Avoid Self-Explanation

You must add comments to the code if you want to explain what you have done. This does not mean you should add self-explanatory comments. These do not add any value to the code. Use comments that help people. For instance:

```
final double PI = 3.14; // This is pi value
    //
```

Do you think the above statement needs a comment? ? Since this holds the value of Pi, the comment does not add any value to the code. It is self-explanatory.

Chapter Six

The Basic Questions

Now that you have an idea of what to expect from a coding interview and what you can do to succeed at the interview, let us look at some common questions asked. It is important to give examples to the interviewer since it will be easier for him to determine if your understanding is correct.

Questions on Algorithms

What are algorithms?

Note: This is an important question, and you need to understand an algorithm and how you should use it. It is easy to build a program only if you know what algorithm you should use.

An algorithm is a set of rules, instructions, or processes any machine or system should follow to solve a problem. It can include the type of operations to use and the variables one should declare. In simple words, an algorithm is a set of rules defining the steps to complete to obtain the desired results.

Note: If you are new to an algorithm, bear in mind that an algorithm is the same as a recipe. Any dish you make will taste good only if the ingredients used are good and added in the right order. In this case, the ingredients are the input variables, and the final dish is the output variable.

What are the characteristics of algorithms?

The characteristics are:

- The algorithm is achievable or feasible
- It is finite
- There is no dependence on the type of programming language to be used
- No ambiguity exists in the steps the machine has to execute
- Well-defined inputs and outputs.

What do you mean when you say an algorithm is feasible?

Algorithms should be simple, generic, and practical. Ensure any programming language can execute this algorithm based on the resources the programming language has available. Do not write an algorithm without knowing how to use a programming language to code it. Write an algorithm based on the information you have about how to use it.

Why should algorithms not depend on programming languages?

No algorithm should have a dependency on a programming language. The instructions should be precise and simple. Ensure you can use any programming language to write your algorithm. As mentioned earlier, the output will be the same.

Why would an ambiguous algorithm affect the performance of the machine?

Every algorithm you write should be clear and unambiguous. Every step should be clear and should only mean one thing. The compiler should never be given the chance to think of two or three different ways to perform a certain step. Every instruction should be clear in every aspect. If the compiler is given too much time to think about the different ways a specific instruction can be performed, it will only increase the compiler time. This would also mean the computer would use too many resources.

What do you mean by well-defined inputs and outputs?

When you make a new dish, you should look at the relevant ingredients and ensure they are exactly what you need to make the dish. This is the same for the inputs you enter when you write an algorithm. If you follow the instructions given in a recipe to the tee, your dish will be exactly what you decided to make. Ensure the algorithm you write will clearly define the type of output you want to obtain. This means you need to define the output clearly.

How would you write the accurate algorithm for any function you want to perform?

The following questions should be answered before you write any algorithm:

- What inputs do you want to use for the algorithm?
- What constraints do you bear in mind when you try to solve this problem?
- What is the desired or expected output?
- What problem are you trying to solve by writing this algorithm?
- What is the solution to the problem based on the constraints?

This is the best way to determine the type of variables the computer has to use and the output you will receive.

What are the characteristics of an effective algorithm?

You can choose an effective algorithm based on the following criteria:

- Assess and understand the computer architecture and the devices used to run the algorithm

- Identify the different constraints you need to consider when developing the algorithm

- Accuracy of the algorithm to ensure you obtain the expected result regardless of the number of times you use the algorithm. An incorrect algorithm will either give you an incorrect output or may not use all input instances

- Define the algorithm's efficiency based on the inputs you will use to obtain the expected output.

What are the advantages of using algorithms?

1. The procedure is precise and definite

2. Algorithms allow you to divide or break the problem into smaller segments, and this makes it easier for a developer or programmer to write this algorithm in the form of a program depending on the type of programming language you want to use

3. It is easy to understand an algorithm, and therefore, it becomes easier for you to identify any errors in the code based on the algorithm you have written

4. An algorithm is a step-by-step representation of the solution for any problem. This means it is easy for anybody to understand an algorithm

5. Algorithms are not dependent on the type of programming language used. This means they are easy for anybody to understand even if they have no knowledge of programming.

What are the disadvantages of algorithms?

1. You cannot use an algorithm to explain or depict a large program

2. It will take a long time to write complex algorithms

3. Since algorithms are not computer programs, you should put extra effort into developing a computer program.

What is a greedy algorithm?

It becomes easier to divide the problem into smaller problems using the greedy algorithm, and finding the right solution to these subproblems. It will then try to look for the optimal solution for the main problem. Having said that, do not expect to find the optimal solution to a problem using this algorithm. Some examples of this algorithm are the Huffman coding problem and counting money.

Give me an example of a greedy algorithm.

Let us consider the Huffman coding problem. The objective is to compress data without losing any information from the set you have. This means you first have to assign values to different input characters. If you use a programming language to replicate this algorithm, the length of the code will vary depending on how often you use the input characters to solve the problem. Every character you use will have a smaller code, but the code's length depends on how often you use the variable or character. When it comes to solving this problem, you need to consider two parts:

1. Developing and creating the Huffman tree

2. Traversing the tree to find the solution

Consider the string "YYYZXXYYZ." If you count the number of characters in this string, the highest frequency is "Y," and the character with the least frequency is "Z." When you write the code using any programming language, the code will be the smallest for Y and the largest for Z. The complexity of assigning code for these characters depends on the character's frequency.

Let us now look at the input and output variables.

Input: For this example, let us look at a string with different characters, say "BCCBEBFFFFADCEFLLKLKKEEBFF"

Output: Let us now assign the code for each of these characters:

```
Data: F, Frequency: 7, Code: 01

Data: L, Frequency: 3, Code: 0001

Data: K, Frequency: 3, Code: 0000

Data: C, Frequency: 3, Code: 101

Data: B, Frequency: 4, Code: 100

Data: D, Frequency: 1, Code: 110
```

Data: E, Frequency: 4, Code: 001

Let us now look at how you can write the algorithm to build the tree:

1. Declare and initialize a string with different characters.

2. Assign codes to each of the characters in the string.

3. Build the Huffman tree.

    a. Define each node in the tree based on the node's character, frequency, and right and left child.

    b. Create the frequency list and store the frequency of every character in the list. The frequency should be assigned to zero for the characters.

    c. For every character in the string, increase the frequency in the list if it is present.

    d. End the loop.

    e. If the frequency is non-zero, add the character to the tree node and assign a priority to the node as Q.

4. If the priority list, Q, is not empty, remove the item from the list and assign it to the left node; else, assign it to the right node.

5. Move across the node to find the code assigned to the character.

6. End the algorithm.

57

If you want to traverse or move across the tree, use the following input:

1. The Huffman tree and the node

2. The code assigned to the node

The output will leave you with the character and the code assigned to this character.

1. If the left child of the node is a null value, then traverse through the right child and assign the code 1

2. If the left child of the node is not a null value, then traverse through the child and assign the code zero

3. Display the characters with their current code

Basic Programming Concepts

Define Boolean logic.

You must learn about AND, OR, NOT, etc., if you wish to combine different values. Using these operators, creating truth tables will become easy Programmers often use a Boolean operator. One of the most important things to consider is that every expression should be evaluated as true or false. You need to determine the syntax to use based on the language you choose to write in.

Can you explain concurrency? How would you use it in code?

The concept of concurrency is quite different from parallel computing. The concepts are similar, but the difference is in parallel computing, the code runs on different processes at the same time. If you use concurrency, the program can be split into different segments, and each segment is executed separately. You can do this even if the program is running and functioning correctly.

Many programming languages use the concept of multithreading, but it is better to use the concept of concurrency to write code. Concurrency ensures fewer errors in the code. For example, if you were to code in C#, use the Task Parallel Library or TPL to add some elements of concurrency to the code. This method uses the CLR thread pool to run multiple processes allowing you to run the program without having to create threads, which is a very costly operation. You can chain various tasks together and run them together to obtain the results.

It is best to use asynchronous code if you want since it allows you to run programs at the same time without hampering the functioning of other code. When you use asynchronous code to make some web service calls, the code runs without blocking the thread. The thread can continue to respond to any other requests while it waits for the first few requests to complete. In the example below, we will see how to use asynchronous code and concurrency to perform functions.

```
public async Task MethodAsync()

{

    Task longRunningTask =
LongRunningTaskAsync();
```

```
... any code here


    int result = await longRunningTask;

    DoSomething(result);

}



public async Task LongRunningTaskAsync() {
// returns an int

    await Task.Delay(1000);

    return 1;

}
```

At times, a programmer may choose to use different pages to access information at the same time. While the compiler fetches a page, it will process it. It is impossible to determine how the pages are processed, and the order in which the compiler performs this function since every language uses the process of concurrency to perform this activity.

When would you choose to use decision or selection statements?

Never write a program that only performs one action. It is important to ensure the code you write is flexible and can be updated to suit other needs if needed. In this scenario, you should write a program with functions performing operations only if the input value is a specific variable. Use different statements, such as selection or if-else statements, to use any input and perform a function or action based on the condition. You can use lists and arrays.

What is immutability?

If you declare some variables as immutable in your code, you cannot change them. Some programming languages allow you to determine the immutability of a variable using specific prefixes. You should, however, ensure you do not have any dependencies on the variable. You can always change the declaration. The example below will look at how to declare variables with immutable properties. We will also declare some fields as immutable.

```
class Person {



    let firstName: String

    let lastName: String



    init(first: String, last: String) {

        firstName = first

        lastName = last

    }



    public func toString() -> String {
```

```
        return "\(self.firstName)
\(self.lastName)";

    }

}


var man = Person(first:"David",
last:"Bolton")

print( man.toString() )
```

The output of the following code is

```
David Bolton.
```

If you want to change the first or last name in the code, the compiler will throw an error. It is important to use immutable variables in the code. Using these variables, the compiler optimizes the output. The immutable data type will never change if you use a multi-threaded programming language. The value of the variable is shared between different modules and threads. If you want to copy the value of an immutable object, you should only copy the reference to the variable but not the actual value or the variable itself.

Explain loops.

Note: Loops are a very important technique you must understand better before an interview. Most programmers use these statements to perform repetitive actions.

Loops allow you to perform repetitive actions if a specific condition is met. The for loop is the most common type of loop or repetition programmers use in their code. Some coders also choose to use the while loop when they code. The while loop does complicate the solution. In most programming languages, the for loop will use the idea of counting the number of iterations. The programming language used determines how the compiler evaluates the iterations. The language used also determines how the compiler evaluates variables.

What is a linked list?

Note: Most programmers worry about using linked lists since they are slightly difficult to understand. It is for this reason you should give the interviewer the right definition so that you can gain some brownie points. The last chapter in the book has an example program using linked lists.

A linked list is a strange concept since the user should know how a pointer can be used in a linked list and how this pointer works. Linked lists combine the functions of an array with pointers and structures. One can say a linked list is like an array of structures. Unlike a data structure, such as an array or list, the user can easily remove the elements of a linked list.

What is a pointer?

Most programming languages use pointers, and these pointers are used to manipulate different variables stored in a computer's memory. You may be wondering why you would want to use a pointer to navigate to a certain part in your memory, but using a pointer allows you to change the value of any variable using an operator or function. Pointers give programming languages more power when compared to other programming languages. It does take some time to understand how to use pointers and what you can do to variables using pointers. You can declare pointers using an asterisk. You have to ensure the compiler doesn't confuse this asterisk with the multiplication operation. Assign a pointer before you use it.

What are safe calls?

Sir Tony Hoare, a computer scientist, once said you should never introduce a null reference to your code since this will only lead to errors in the output. Accessing a variable using a null reference will lead to an exception unless you have the right handler in place. The program or system will otherwise crash. It is best to use programming languages with exception handlers so that you can avoid recurring errors in your code. Some high-level programming languages, such as C, cannot identify null pointers in the code, and this can lead to errors in the output.

Numerous programming languages include safety checks, and these prevent any null reference errors. For example, in C#, you can avoid blocks of code if you have the right exception handler in place. You have to use a condition to explain to the compiler which lines of code it should avoid. This reduces the number of lines the compiler should run in the code.

Consider the following example:

```
int? count = customers?[0]?.Orders?.Count();
```

The symbol '?' indicates to the compiler to set the value to zero if the customer variable defined in the code has a null value. Otherwise, the compiler will call upon the Count() function. If you use the function, you have to declare the variable to hold a null value so you do not have an error when the code is run.

Questions on Variables

What are variables?

The objective of any method or function written is to obtain a result or output. You will not get the right output if you do not use the right variables in the code. The programs you develop may also be of no use to you. For example, how would it feel if you developed a program to obtain the output of a mathematical function but did not receive the output because you missed a variable in the code? It is for this reason you have to include variables in the code. These are the most important aspects of any programming language. The variables you use in the code, their type, and the method used to declare and initialize the variable will differ between programming languages.

What are random and scaling numbers?

Most high-level programming languages use different types of libraries. Using these libraries, you can generate random numbers. If you use a programming language without this feature, it is best to use integers to perform different methods and functions. This will, however, not serve the purpose. Therefore, learning how to obtain random numbers and use the necessary functions to scale them is important. Through scaling, you can ensure shapes on a screen will always either increase or decrease in the same size.

Random numbers can also be used just because you want to, especially when you use different data structures. When you add a degree of randomness to these numbers, you can make the numbers look natural. For instance, if you want to draw a tree or any other object on the screen, you can use the recursion concept to do this. If you do not add some randomness to the code, the object you draw will not look like it.

Many functions in different programming languages allow you to create pseudorandom numbers. These numbers can be distributed uniformly within a range. Bear in mind this is not something you are required to do.

What is a string? Tell me the different ways you can use the variable.

Strings are a common data type most programmers work with, and this is often used in any text manipulation program. We will look at what text manipulation is later in this chapter. You can define a string using an array or any other data structure but define it as a structure of characters. For instance,

```
Char name1[] = "Emma";
```

Using the above line, you can create a string variable called name1, and this variable holds the value Emma. Since you have defined the variable as an array, the value will be saved as 'E,' 'm,' 'm', and 'a.' Alternatively, you can write the value using the following format:

```
Char name1[] = { 'E', 'm', 'm', 'a'};
```

It is important to keep the following points in mind regarding strings:

- Different functions can be used to manipulate strings.

- Strings end with the null character that is defined in the library class stdio.h. `

- You can read strings using scanf() or get(). String values can be displayed using the printf() function.

- Any string ends with a null character.

Can you explain text manipulation? How does this help you in a program?

Note: Text manipulation is a key concept, and most people writing code want to learn how to manipulate characters and strings. You need to understand these concepts well.

Text is stored in numerals based on the ASCII code. Therefore, it is important to know how to convert any character into its ASCII code and vice versa. You can also use this number to check if the characters are upper or lower case. Using the ASCII code, you can create ciphers using bitwise EOR.

You can also break or divide strings using the left() and right() functions, and this allows you to perform different types of tasks.

You can create anagrams or display the required texts on the screen. The text manipulation functions in any programming language allow you to change the case of any letter and format text so it looks a certain way when you build the code or program. You can do this to improve how your program appears.

Questions on Operators

What are the different operators one can use in programming?

You can manipulate and perform different operators on variables and data using an operator.

Note: When you tell the interviewer about the different operators used in programming, also mention to him how you can use the operator. Logical and relational operators are extremely important, so it is best to begin with these. Arithmetic operators are self-explanatory, but you can give the interviewer an overview of the same.

Logical

Operator	Description
&& (logical and)	returns false if either value is zero, and true otherwise
|| (logical or)	returns false if the value is zero, and true otherwise

! (logical not)	returns true if the value of the condition is false, and false otherwise

Relational

There are several relational operators in a programming language:

Operator	Description
== (equal to)	checks if the values of the operands are equal; evaluates true if they are
!= (not equal to)	checks if the values of the operands are equal; evaluates true if not
> (greater than)	checks if the left operand is greater than the right; evaluates true if it is
< (less than)	checks if the left operand is less than the right; evaluates true if it is
>= (greater than or equal to)	checks if the left operand is greater than or the same as the right; evaluates true if it is
<= (less than or equal to)	checks if the left operand is less than or the same as the right; evaluates true if it is

Arithmetic

These are used for mathematical expressions in much the same way you used the same symbols at school:

Operator	Description
+	Addition for adding values on the left or right of the operator
-	Subtraction for subtracting the right operand from the left
*	Multiplication for multiplying values on the left or right of the operator
/	Division for dividing the left operand by the right operand
%	Modulus, the remainder of the division of the left operand by the right operand
++	Increment, for increasing an operand value by 1
--	Decrement, for decreasing an operand value by 1

Assignment

Operator	Description
=	assigns the value from the right operand to the left
+=	adds the value of the right operand to the left and assigns the result to the left
-=	subtracts the right from the left operand and assigns the result to the left
*=	multiplies the right with the left operand and assigns the result to the left
/=	divides the left operand with the right and assigns the result to the left
%=	takes the modulus of two operands and assigns the result to the left
<<=	left shift and assignment
>>=	right shift and assignment

Explain operator precedence.

Every programming language has operator precedence to determine how expressions are evaluated by looking at the variables within them. Some operators have higher precedence than others, such as multiplication over addition. For instance:

```
x = 6 + 2 * 3
```

Here, if you calculate the value of x, you may say 24. Since multiplication is higher in the precedence order, the processor or compiler will calculate this as 2*3 and then add the 6. Here, the operators are in order of their precedence from highest to lowest.

In any expression, those operators with the highest precedence will be the first ones evaluated:

Category	Operator	Associativity
Postfix	>() [] . (dot operator)	Left to right
Unary	>++ - - ! ~	Right to left
Multiplicative	>* /	Left to right
Additive	>+ -	Left to right
Shift	>>> >>> <<	Left to right
Relational	>> >= < <=	Left to right
Equality	>== !=	Left to right

Logical AND	>&&	Left to right
Logical OR	>||	Left to right
Conditional	?:	Right to left
Assignment	>= += -= *= /= %=	
	>>= <<= &= ^= |=	Right to left

Other Questions

What are data structures?

Every programming language uses a combination of different variables, and you can convert variables into different data structures. A structure is like a record in a database since it can be used to describe numerous entities at the same time. As a programmer, you can determine how to declare and initialize a data structure. Consider the following example:

```
struct example

{

  int a;

char b;

float c;

}
```

In the above structure, we see three variables. Each variable is assigned a specific data type. Using this function, you can create a

73

structure with three variables, but you do not necessarily have to declare these variables. If you would like to declare the variables, you will have to increase the number of lines in your code. A structure can also be used to work on different databases based on the type of programming language you are working with. You should learn everything about different programming languages and structures, especially how to use them to write code.

Give me a few examples of error handling.

One of the easiest things to do is to use certain keywords, like null, to handle errors and exceptions in your code. Every programming language uses keywords differently. Ensure you have the right error handling code in place, but if the code obscures the logic, then do not include the error handling code in your main code. Here are some tips you need to bear in mind:

- Instead of pointing the compiler to a block of error code in the program, it is best to throw an exception. If you do not point the compiler to an error code in the program, you should indicate to the compiler to look for the issue in the code and debug it. If you do write the code, make sure you know where you have added this code. Throw exceptions when there is an error in the code to avoid issues with the debugging of the code

- If you add an exception to the code, you should provide the compiler with enough information to allow you to determine the position of the error in the code. Create an informative error message and pass this message to the exception. It is also important to ensure the operation you are performing in the code did not work the way it is expected to work

- You can include the catch keyword in the code to identify errors, but it is important to use the keyword in the right location. You should also use the 'try' keyword to identify the error in the code. Start the error handling code with a try-catch-finally statement while you write the code

Note: It is important for you to define exceptions in the code based on the needs of the function. Having said that, it is also important for you to determine how you want to classify errors in the code. Do you want to classify the error based on its type, such as programming error, network failure, or incorrect arguments? Or do you want to classify errors based on their source? Or will you classify the errors based on how the compiler identifies these errors?

What are some of the common error messages?

Simple programs are easy to compile. You may not have errors in the code if you have stuck to the algorithm and used the right variable to code. This should not make you overconfident since this is usually not the case. As a programmer, you will spend most of your time dealing with certain flaws in the program you have written. The process of fixing the errors is called debugging. This section will look at different ways to handle errors in any program you have written.

Editing and Recompiling

You may have issues with spelling in your code. This may not seem like a big issue, but the compiler will throw an error if you have the wrong words in the code. This indicates you have to go through the code to fix the error. Do not worry about dealing with too many errors since this is the only way you learn. You need to go through the following steps to overcome any errors in your code. You need to follow the steps given below to re-run the code.

- Re-edit the source code and save the file to the disk

- Recompile the code

- Run the program

You may still have many errors while reediting your code. Do not worry since you will get to step 3 once you identify how to work with and edit the errors in programs.

Re-edit the source code

You can change the source code file as often as needed. Often, these changes are necessary to overcome any error messages the compiler may throw your way. There are times when you would want to change the code by changing the message on the screen or by adding a feature.

Recompile

In this step, you have to run the program one more time and compile it once you have made changes to the code. Link the program to the compiler. Since the code is different, you should send the code to the compiler only after you link the code. If the compiler throws an error again, you must repeat the first step. To recompile the program one more time, enter the following code in the command prompt to trigger the compiler:

```
gcc hello.c -0 hello
```

If no error message pops up, pat yourself on the back. You no longer have errors in your code.

Can you write a sample error handling code?

Some programming languages allow you to convert blocks of existing code into exception or error handling code. In the example below, we will see how this can be done:

```
class LocalPort {

   private let innerPort: ACMEPort   func
open() throws {

      do {

        try innerPort.open()

      } catch let error as DeviceResponseError
{

        throw
PortDeviceFailure.portDeviceFailure(error:
error)

      } catch let error as
ATM1212UnlockedError {
```

```
    throw
PortDeviceFailure.portDeviceFailure(error:
error)

    } catch let error as GMXError {

    throw
PortDeviceFailure.portDeviceFailure(error:
error)

    }

  }

}
```

What is the null keyword? How do you use it?

If you add a null keyword into a method, the code you have written
will become impossible to debug. It is important for you to avoid
this. Adding null values to the error handling code increases work
for you. If the output is a null value, you have to struggle to identify
where the null value came up in your code.

```
// Un-swifty, but matches code in book

func register(item: Item?) {

  if item != nil {

    let registry: ItemRegistry? =
persitentStore.getItemRegistry()

    if registry != nil {

      let existingItem =
registry.getItem(item.getId())
```

```
        if
existingItem.getBillingPeriod().hasRetailOwn
er()) {

        existingItem.register(item)
```

Chapter Seven

Questions on Debugging

In this chapter, we will look at some questions interviewers may ask about debugging. They may also give you a piece of code and ask you to identify the errors or debug the code.

This is a task any coder should do on a regular basis. Therefore, it is important for you to gather as much information as you can about this topic. They often tend to ask you how you would debug the code you have written. Some points you can mention while you have a conversation with the interviewer:

- As a programmer, you need to be prepared for errors to exist in the code

- Do not spend too much time trying to debug the code and identifying issues in it

- Use a formulated approach to identify the errors in the code

- Consider the algorithm, design, and correctness of the code to prepare yourself for the arduous task

Let us now consider some questions the interviewer may ask based on the points above.

How Would You Explain the Algorithm and Assess the Design of the Code?

It is important to understand the algorithm fully before you write any code. Otherwise, you will do something you never wanted to in the first place. You cannot test the module if you do not understand the design since you have no idea what the objective of the module is.

If you are using another's code as a reference, review the algorithm, design, and comments to understand the objective of the code. If you do not know how the algorithm functions, you cannot develop effective test cases, and this is true when you use data structures in your code. This means you cannot determine if the algorithm works as expected.

What Methods Will You Use to Check the Correctness or Accuracy of the Code?

Different methods can be used to debug code and determine if the information written is correct and the compiler runs without throwing errors.

Note: Mention some of these methods to the interviewer so he is aware of your knowledge. He needs to know you are aware of what should be done so he knows where your strengths lie.

Code Tracing

You can detect errors in code easily by tracing the execution of different functions and modules in the code. It is especially important to do this when calls are made to the function or module in different parts of the program. As the programmer, you have to trace how the functions and modules work.

If you want this process to be effective, you should trace the modules and functions by assuming other functions and procedures in the code work accurately. You must deal with different layers or levels of inheritance and abstraction when performing code tracing. Bear in mind you cannot find all errors through tracing. This process, however, improves your understanding of the algorithm used.

Peer Reviews

It is best to have another person who is well versed in writing code assess and examine the code you have written. If you want the review to be effective, you have to ensure the peer has the required information and knowledge to check the code. It is important to give the peer the code with the comments so he knows exactly what to expect in the code.

If you want to make it easier for the peer, you can explain the code to them and tell them how the algorithm functions. If the reviewer disagrees or does not understand some parts of the implementation, you need to discuss it with him until you both reach an agreement. The objective of the peer should be to detect the errors in the code. It becomes easier to correct them if identified correctly.

You can identify these issues yourself when you proof the code. Having said that, it is useful if you have someone from the outside looking at the code and identifying some blind spots in the code. Peer reviews will take time, so ensure you restrict the reviews to only those sections of code you want to be assessed and not the entire code.

Proof of Correctness

The best way to identify any error in the code is to examine the algorithm used and use different methods to validate the correctness of the algorithm. For example, if you know the preconditions, terminating conditions, invariants, and postconditions in any loop statement used, you can perform simple checks in the code. Ask the following questions to determine the correctness of the code:

1. If the compiler has entered the loop without throwing any error, does it mean the invariant used is accurate?

2. If the statements in the loop body do not throw an error, does it mean the loop has worked well and will terminate without any error?

3. If the loop is nearing the end, does it mean the compiler will move towards the postcondition?

These questions may not help you determine if there are errors in the code, but they give you an understanding of the algorithm.

Why Do You Think It Is Important to Anticipate Errors?

It is fortunate to have errors in the code since there is a possibility you may use incorrect pointers and variables in the code. You may also forget to call or use certain functions and parameters in the code. We also make mistakes when it comes to tracing the code, and peer reviews may not catch all the errors in the code. You have to be prepared for these errors in the code and use the error handling techniques we discussed earlier in the book.

Why Is It Important to Have Comments in Your Code?

It is important to understand how to write comments effectively. Most people wonder if they should add a lot of comments to explain every line of code. The issue with comments is you often forget to update them. You may want to change the code, but it is possible you may ignore the comments. This would mean the comments reflect the older code.

A difficult thing to do is to educate a programmer on how to write comments in the code. The moment you change the code, you should also change the comments. You should never forget about updating comments since this could lead to issues in the functioning of the code. You should look at the comments as documentation. Maintain these comments since it is the only way to explain what your code does. Ensure you add comments to express exactly what is happening in the code.

Should You Add Comments Everywhere in the Code?

No, every programmer needs to ensure he only adds comments to the code where necessary. It is important to remember the following:

1. Do not add comments only because you are expected to. This will affect the look of the code

2. If you add unnecessary comments, you will have irrelevant information in your code

3. At times, such comments can make it hard for you to read the code or even understand it

Why Is Indenting a Comment Important?

Comments are the best way to explain your intent behind writing the code. This does not mean you should use comments to explain every line of code. Your code should do it. It is important to explain what it is you want to do in the code. Sometimes, you cannot express the intent behind writing the code. It is for this reason you should add some comments to explain why you took a specific action. Some methods may have been used to deal with external library issues, or you had to incorporate odd requests. No matter what it is, it's important to explain these sections in better detail.

```
// Code to check if the input variables are
valid

function is_valid($first_name, $last_name,
$age) {

    if (

            !ctype_alpha($_POST['first_name'])
    OR

            !ctype_alpha($_POST['last_name']) OR

            !ctype_digit($_POST['age'])

            ) {

            return false;

    }

    return true;

}

switch(animal) {

    case 1:

        cat();

        // falls through

    case 2:
```

```
        dog();

        break;

    }
```

What to Keep in Mind When You Test the Code You Have Written?

The following rules need to be kept in mind if you choose to perform a TTD test on the code you write:

1. You should create a prototype of the code and write the test code. Run this code and compile it to see if it works well. You need to do this before you write the production code

2. Ensure you do not write a big code because it is possible the test will fail. Use smaller segments of code as test code, so it becomes easier to correct the code

3. Rewrite the test code if there are failures, compile the code and then write the production code

When you perform tests on the code, write the production code at the same time to ensure the code you write is accurate.

How to Keep the Code Clean

Ensure the tests you run are clean of any errors. If you have a test code filled with bugs, do not run the test since it is of no use to you. Bear in mind the test code should change as often as the production code changes. If the tests are dirty, it will be hard to change them. You have to design the test in the right manner. You have to be careful and think through the process. Ensure the test code is clean and a replica of the production code.

What Are the Important Characteristics of Tests?

Note: This is an important question, as you should know what to do when it comes to preparing test codes. You should know what to include and remove from your test code, to validate the program you have written.

There are five characteristics you need to consider when writing testing code.

Self-Validating: Every test should have a Boolean output to help you determine if the test works the way it should. Ensure a user doesn't go through the log to verify the code you have written.

Independent: None of the tests you run should have a dependence on each other. Run the tests in different orders to ensure the code works regardless of the type of environment it is in.

Timely: Ensure the tests you write can compile in a few seconds. Write the test code before you write the production code, so you can tweak the production code and run it without errors. If you start writing tests after you begin writing the production code, you cannot update it, so it has no errors.

Repeatable: You should try to repeat every test you perform in any environment. If you write a test code but it cannot perform well in other environments, you need to determine why it fails.

Fast: Ensure every test you perform is fast. If the test is slow, you may not want to run it frequently because it will take up too much time. A slow test may not help you with identifying issues in your code.

Chapter Eight

Questions on Data Structures

In this chapter, we will look at some of the common questions an interviewer may ask about data structures. They often ask you about how you would define or create a new structure in the code and what steps you need to follow to create it.

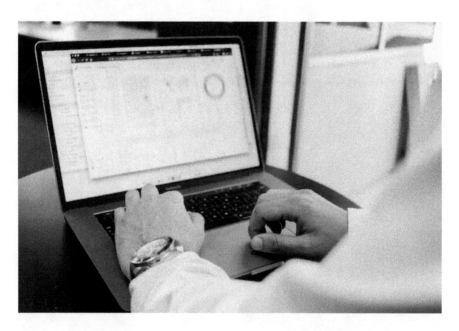

Note: The programs written in this chapter are compatible with C and C++. The examples in this chapter are based on the following scenario - Let us assume you want to arrange the bookshelf in your library. We will see how you can use a data structure to track different attributes of every book. For this example, we will look at the following attributes:

1. Book ID

2. Book title

3. Genre

4. Author

What Is Data Structure?

A structure allows you to combine different variables and data types. You can use a structure to define or represent records. Some examples include arrays and lists.

How Do You Create a Data Structure? Give Me an Example of the Process You Will Follow.

Before you define any data structure, it is important to use the struct statement to create the structure in the program. Bear in mind the struct statement works only in C and C++ languages. However, other programming languages use a different statement. You can also define the number of elements or members in the code.

Use the following syntax to define the structure in your code:

```
struct [structure tag] {

    member definition;
```

```
member definition;

...

member definition;

} [one or more structure variables];
```

Using the structure tag is not necessary when you use the struct statement. Use the variable definition method to describe every member you want to use in the structure. If you are unsure of how to describe the data, learn how to do this to avoid making mistakes. For instance, you can use the method int i to define an integer variable. The section before the semicolon in the struct syntax is also optional. It is best to keep this in the program since you define the variables you want to use in the structure. Continuing with the example above, we will define the book structure using the following lines of code.

```
struct Books {

    int book_id;

    char book_title[50];

    char genre[50];

    char author[100];

} book;
```

How Do You Access the Variables within the Data Structure?
It is easy to access data structure members using a 'full stop.' This full stop is known as the member access operator. It is used as a

break or period between the data structure members and the names of variables. Ensure to enter the variable name you want to access. You can define the variable of the entire structure using the struct keyword. Consider the following lines of code to understand how you can use structures. We will be continuing the example mentioned at the start of the chapter.

```cpp
#include <iostream>

#include <cstring>

using namespace std;

struct Books {

    int book_id;

    char book_title[60];

    char genre[60];

    char author[40];

};

int main() {

    struct Books Book1; // Using this
statement, you can declare the first
variable called Book1 in the data structure.

    struct Books Book2; // Using this
statement, you can declare the first
variable called Book2 in the data structure.
```

```
// The next lines of code will instruct the
compiler on how to add details to the first
variable

    Book1.book_id = 1001;

    strcpy( Book1.book_title, "Eragon");

    strcpy( Book 1.genre, " Fantasy");

    strcpy( Book1.author, "Christopher
Paolini");

// The next lines add data to the second
variable

    Book2.book_id = 1002;

    strcpy( Book2.book_title, "Eldest");

    strcpy( Book2.genre, "Fantasy");

    strcpy( Book2.author, "Christopher
Paolini");

// We will use the next lines of code to
print the details of the first and second
variables in the data structure

    cout << "Book 1 id: " << Book1.book_id
<<endl;

    cout << "Book 1 title: " <<
Book1.book_title <<endl;

    cout << "Book 1 genre: " << Book1.genre
<<endl;
```

```cpp
    cout << "Book 1 author: " << Book1.author
<<endl;

    cout << "Book 2 id: " << Book2.book_id
<<endl;

    cout << "Book 2 title: " <<
Book2.book_title <<endl;

    cout << "Book 2 genre: " << Book2.genre
<<endl;

    cout << "Book 2 author: " << Book2.author
<<endl;

    return 0;

}
```

The code above will give you the following output:

```
Book 1 id: 1001

Book 1 title: Eragon

Book 1 genre: Fantasy

Book 1 author: Christopher Paolini

Book 2 id: 1002

Book 2 title: Eldest

Book 2 genre: Fantasy

Book 2 author: Christopher Paolini
```

Can You Use Structures as Arguments? If Yes, How Would You Use Them?

Yes, a data structure can also be called as an argument in a function. This works in the same way you would pass any variable or pointer as a parameter in the function. To do this, you should only access the variables the way we did in the above example.

```
#include <iostream>

#include <cstring>

 using namespace std;

 struct Books {

    int book_id;

    char book_title[60];

    char genre[60];

    char author[40];

};

 int main() {

    struct Books Book1; // Using this
statement, you can declare the first
variable called Book1 in the data structure.

    struct Books Book2; // Using this
statement, you can declare the first
variable called Book2 in the data structure.
```

```
// The next lines of code will instruct the
compiler on how to add details to the first
variable

    Book1.book_id = 1001;

    strcpy( Book1.book_title, "Eragon");

    strcpy( Book1.genre, " Fantasy");

    strcpy( Book1.author, "Christopher
Paolini");

// The next lines add data to the second
variable

    Book2.book_id = 1002;

    strcpy( Book2.book_title, "Eldest");

    strcpy( Book2.genre, "Fantasy");

    strcpy( Book2.author, "Christopher
Paolini");

// Let us now look at how you can specify
the details of the second variable

    Book2.book_id = 130000;

    strcpy( Book2.book_title, "Harry Potter
and the Chamber of Secrets");

    strcpy( Book2.genre, "Fiction");

    strcpy( Book2.author, "JK Rowling");
```

```cpp
// The next statements are to print the
details of the first and second variables in
the structure

    printBook( Book1 );

    printBook( Book2 );

    return 0;

}

void printBook(struct Books book ) {

    cout << "Book id: " << book.book_id
<<endl;

    cout << "Book title: " << book.book_title
<<endl;

    cout << "Book genre: " << book.genre
<<endl;

    cout << "Book author: " <<
book.author<<endl;

}
```

When you compile the code written above, you receive the following output:

```
Book 1 id: 120000

Book 1 title: Harry Potter and the
Philosopher's Stone

Book 1 genre: Fiction
```

```
Book 1 author: JK Rowling

Book 2 id: 130000

Book 2 title: Harry Potter and the Chamber
of Secrets

Book 2 genre: Fiction

Book 2 author: JK Rowling
```

How Do You Refer to Structures in a Program? Which Method Would You Use?

You can also refer to structures using pointers, and you can use a pointer similar to how you would define a pointer for regular variables.

```
struct Books *struct_pointer;
```

When you use the above statement, you can use the pointer variable defined to store the address of the variables in the structure.

```
struct_pointer = &Book1;
```

You can also use a pointer to access one or all members of the structure. To do this, you need to use the -> operator:

```
struct_pointer->title;
```

Let us rewrite the example above to indicate a member or the entire structure using a pointer.

```
#include <iostream>

#include <cstring>
```

```cpp
using namespace std;

void printBook( struct Books *book );

struct Books {

    int book_id;

    char book_title[50];

    char genre[50];

    char author[100];

};

 int main() {

   struct Books Book1; // This is where you
declare the variable Book1 in the Book
structure

    struct Books Book2; // This is where you
declare the variable Book2 in the Book
structure

// Let us now look at how you can specify
the details of the first variable

   Book1.book_id = 1001;

   strcpy( Book1.book_title, "Eragon");

   strcpy( Book1.genre, "Fantasy");

    strcpy( Book1.author, "Christopher
Paolini");
```

```cpp
// Let us now look at how you can specify
the details of the second variable

    Book2.book_id = 1002;

    strcpy( Book2.book_title, "Eldest");

    strcpy( Book2.genre, "Fantasy");

    strcpy( Book2.author, "Christopher
Paolini");

// The next statements are to print the
details of the first and second variables in
the structure

    printBook( Book1 );

    printBook( Book2 );

    return 0;

}

// We will now use a function to accept a
structure pointer as its parameter.

void printBook( struct Books *book ) {

    cout << "Book id: " << book->book_id
<<endl;

    cout << "Book title: " << book-
>book_title <<endl;

    cout << "Book genre: " << book-
>genre<<endl;
```

```
    cout << "Book author: " << book->author
<<endl;

}
```

When you write the above code, you obtain the following output:

```
Book id: 1001

Book title: Eragon

Book genre: Fantasy

Book author: Christopher Paolini

Book id: 1002

Book title: Eldest

Book genre: Fantasy

Book author: Christopher Paolini
```

Can You Give Me an Example Using the Typedef Keyword?

If you cannot define the data structure easily using the above methods, use an alias structure to define the structure. Consider the following example:

```
typedef struct {

    int book_id;

    char book_title[50];

    char genre[50];

    char author[100];
```

```
} Books;
```

Using this process to define the structure is easier since you define the variables used in the structure without using the struct keyword.

```
Books Book1, Book2;
```

Bear in mind a typedef key is not required to define any data structure. You can use it to define any regular variable, as well.

```
typedef long int *pint32;

pint32 x, y, z;
```

The above lines of code show the compiler points to the x, y, and z variables.

Chapter Nine

Questions on Arrays

A rrays are a type of data structure and coders use them a lot. These structures are used to perform different functions. In this chapter, we will look at some common questions interviewers ask during coding interviews.

What Is an Array?

Arrays are collections of variables with the same data type. Every element is assigned an index, and it is best to use these indices to look up the elements in the array. For example, you can create random numbers, so if you want any random item like the day of the week, you can use the index to pull out the random number.

An array is also known as a multivariable since it allows you to store different variables of the same data type together. You can declare arrays in your program the same way you declare other variables in the program:

```
float array1[10];
```

In the example above, we assign an array with the length 10, indicating it can hold 10 values. You can define or add values to the array using the following line:

```
Float array1[] = {53.0, 88.0, 96.7, 93.1, 89.5};
```

Does Every Programming Language Support the Use of Arrays?

Some programming languages do not support the use of data structures, such as arrays. You can, however, replicate the functionalities of an array using lists or tuples. You can use binary trees in an array if the array is sparsely populated. It is messy to do this, but it is easier to do this if you want to use different types of data. JavaScript allows you to use the array index as a Boolean operator, and this means you can use various binary expressions to evaluate the condition. This makes it easier to select the values without using any conditional statements.

What Are Some Important Characteristics of Arrays?

Note: You may have identified other characteristics of arrays. The ones listed below are the most common and important ones for a coder to remember. These characteristics help you use elements in the array as an argument in a function or a calculation.

- You can refer to every element in the array as an independent variable when you use it in a function or module. The items in the array are known as elements

- Every element is given a specific position, and this position is known as the index. The index of the first element in the array is zero.

Note: In the example above, the first number, 53.0, is at the position zero

- You can assign the values to the array the same way you assign values to regular variables

- Every program has a fixed array size, and when you determine the dimension of an array by assigning the array a length

Can You Search in and Sort Arrays? What Are Searching and Sorting Algorithms?

Yes, we can. As the name suggests, a searching algorithm is used to find an element in any data structure and retrieve the element and its location from the structure. Sorting algorithms can be used to sort the information in an array either in ascending or descending order. Different sorting algorithms can arrange a given list of elements or array based on the comparison operator used while defining the algorithm. This comparison operator will decide the order of the elements in the new data structure.

Explain the Different Types of Search Algorithms.

There are two types of search algorithms:

Sequential Search

A sequential search is one where the algorithm traverses through the data structure in a sequential manner to look for the target element. It will search through each element in the data set. An example of this algorithm is the linear search algorithm.

Interval Search

An interval search algorithm searches for the element in a sorted data structure. This means you first use a sorting algorithm on the data structure before you perform an interval search. This type of searching algorithm is effective since it searches for the target at the center of the structure. An example of this type of algorithm is the binary search algorithm, and we will look at this in further detail later in the book.

What Is In-Place Sorting?

If you only want to change a given input or reorder the elements in the input, you can use an in-place sorting algorithm. This algorithm will only sort the list of elements in the array by changing the order of the elements within the same list. For example, you can use the selection sort and insertion sort algorithms to sort a list of elements. Merge sort, and other sorting algorithms are not in-place sorting algorithms.

What Are External and Internal Sorting?

The external sorting algorithm does not use a lot of space in the memory. The elements in the array are not loaded into the memory; therefore, this sorting mechanism is often used to sort large volumes of data. Merge sort is an example of an external sorting algorithm; we will look at this in further detail later in the book. Unlike the external sorting algorithm, an internal sorting algorithm uses a lot of space in the memory.

What Is the Difference between Linear and Sequential Search Algorithms?

A linear search does not require you to sort the array; it scans every item in the array to search for the element. It does not exclude any element in the array, either. This means the time taken by the compiler to search for an element is directly proportional to the number of elements in the data structure. For example, the algorithm will take less time to search for the element if there are only 5 elements in the array but will take longer if there are 15 elements in the array. A binary search, on the other hand, reduces the time taken to search for the element in the array. The following are some of the most common differences between sequential and search algorithms.

- You should sort the array before using the binary search algorithm, but this is not required for a linear search algorithm

- Linear search follows the sequential process while the binary search algorithm will look at the data randomly

- The binary search algorithm performs comparisons based on the segment, while the linear search will perform an equality comparison

In the final chapter of the book, we will look at some programs you can consider in case the interviewer asks you to code

Chapter Ten

Questions on
Decisions and Selections

Decision Making

This is a key piece of programming, and it is important for a programmer to know how to use decision-making statements to perform certain functions. The structures of decision-making statements include at least one condition the compiler should evaluate before it executes the other statements in the decision block. You may also include other statements to execute if the condition is false. The following are the decision-making statements in most programming languages:

?: Operator

We already touched on this earlier. The?: is a conditional operator you can use instead of an if...else statement, and its format looks something like:

State1? State2 : State3 ;

State1, State2, and State3 are all expressions – do note the use of the colon and its placement.

To work out what the value of the entire expression is, State1 is evaluated first:

If State1 has a value of True, the value of State2 will then be the value of the entire expression

If State1 evaluates to false, then State3 will be evaluated, and the value of State3 will be the value of the whole expression.

If Statement

The if statement is the most common decision-making statement used in programming. The condition has a Boolean expression and one or more statements in the body.

If Else Statement

This statement may be succeeded by an else statement, which is optional, which will execute should the Boolean expression evaluate false

Nested if

If you want to test many conditions, use a nested if statement since you can include multiple if statements and one else statement.

Switch Statement

The statement for use when you want to test a variable for equality against a list of given values

Loop Statements

If you want to execute statements numerous times in some lines of code, use loops. Most programming languages have three common loops:

1. For loop

2. While loop

3. Do While loop

For Loop

A for loop executes a statement numerous times depending on the condition stated in the parameters. The loop variable controls the number of times the loop runs. The syntax of this loop is:

```
for (initialization; condition; update)
```

```
{

    Body;

}
```

In the for loop, the loop variable is initialized in the parameters of the function, and the value is either increased or decreased within the body of the loop. The condition in the function above will result in a Boolean output – either true or false, and it determines the number of times the loop runs for. If the condition returns false, the loop will break, and the statements after the loop are executed. If the condition does not break, the loop continues to run indefinitely.

Consider the following example of a for loop where we want to print numbers 0 – 10:

```
for (int i = 0; i <= 10; i++)

{

Console.Write(i + " ");

}
```

You can use the loop to perform complicated functions. For example, you can calculate the power (m) of a number (n).

```
Console.Write("n = ");

int n = int.Parse(Console.ReadLine());

Console.Write("m = ");

int m = int.Parse(Console.ReadLine());
```

```
decimal result = 1;

for (int i = 0; i < m; i++)

{

result *= n;

}

Console.WriteLine("n^m = " + result);
```

In the above code, we are calculating the power of the number within the body of the loop. The condition we have set against the power (m). For loops can also have two variables defined and initialized within the condition.

```
for (int small=1, large=10; small<large;
small++, large--)

{

Console.WriteLine(small + " " + large);

}
```

While Loop

Using the while loop, you can repeat one or more statements in the body of the loop depending on the condition. The condition is tested before the loop body is executed.

The syntax of the loop is as follows:

```
while (condition)

{
```

```
    Body;

}
```

Consider the example below where we want to print the numbers 0 – 9 on the output window.

```
// Initializing the counter variable

int count = 0;

// Setting the loop with the required
condition

while (count <= 9)

{

// Printing the variable on the output
screen

Console.WriteLine("Number :  " + count);

// Incremental operator

counter++;

}
```

The code will give out the following result:

```
Number: 0

Number: 1

Number: 2

Number: 3
```

```
Number:  4

Number:  5

Number:  6

Number:  7

Number:  8

Number:  9
```

Let us now look at how to calculate the sum of numbers 1 – 10.

```
int count = 0;

int sum = 0;

while (count <= 10)

{

sum=sum+count;

count++;

}

Console.WriteLine("The sum is" + sum);
```

You can do this in different ways depending on whether you want to use loops or not. We can also use the while loop to work on other mathematical calculations. The program below checks whether a number entered is a prime number or not.

```
Console.Write("Enter a positive number:  ");

int num = int.Parse(Console.ReadLine());
```

```
int divider = 2; //stores the value of the
potential divisor

int maxDivider = (int)Math.Sqrt(num);

bool prime = true;

while (prime && (divider <= maxDivider))

{

if (num % divider == 0)

{

prime = false;

}

divider++;

}

Console.WriteLine("Prime? " + prime);
```

Do While Loop

The do...while loop is like the while loop with one exception; the loop body is executed before the condition is tested. This means the loop will execute once, even if the condition you have entered is false.

The syntax of the loop is as follows:

```
do

{
```

```
Body;

} while (condition);
```

Once the statements in the body are run, the condition is checked. If the condition is true, then the loop runs again. This function is repeated until the condition is false. The body of the loop is executed at least once since the condition is checked only after the body is executed.

In the example below, we will calculate the factorial of a number.

```
using System;

using System.Numerics;

class Factorial

{

static void Main()

{

Console.Write("n = ");

int n = int.Parse(Console.ReadLine());

BigInteger factorial = 1;

do

{

factorial *= n;

n--;
```

```
} while (n > 0);

Console.WriteLine("n! = " + factorial);

}

}
```

If you run the program now, you can get the factorial of any number of your choosing.

Loop Control Statements

Loop control statements are used to change the normal sequence of execution. When the execution leaves its scope, i.e., it finishes what it set out to do, all the objects automatically created in the scope are then destroyed.

The following control statements are supported in most programming languages:

Break Statement

This operator can be used to break out of a loop. There are times when we may write an incorrect code, and the loop will run indefinitely. The break operator comes in handy at such times since it will automatically bring you out of the loop. This statement can only be written inside the loop if you wish to terminate the iteration from taking place. The code after the break statement is not executed. The following example will show you the code used to calculate a number's factorial.

```
int n = int.Parse(Console.ReadLine());
```

```
// "decimal" is the biggest data type and
holds integer values

decimal factorial = 1;

// Perform an "infinite loop"

while (true)

{

if (n<=1)

{

    break;

}

factorial *= n;

n--;

}

Console.WriteLine("n! = " + factorial);
```

We have initialized a variable called factorial to read variables from
1 – n in the console. Since the condition is true, this creates an
endless loop. Here the break statement will stop the loop from
functioning when the value of n is less than or equal to 1. The loop
will continue to run if the condition in the if statement does not
hold true.

foreach loop

The foreach loop is an extension of the for loop in some programming languages, such as C, C++, and C#, but is a well-known loop. It is also used by PHP and VB programmers. This loop iterates and performs operations on all elements of an array or list. It will operate on all the variables even if the list or array is not indexed. The syntax of the loop is as follows:

```
foreach (type variable in the collection)

    {

        Body;

    }
```

A foreach loop is like the for loop, but most programmers prefer this type of loop since it saves writing a code to go over all the elements in the list. Consider the following example to see how a foreach loop works:

```
int[] numbers = { 2, 3, 5, 7, 11, 13, 17, 19
};

foreach (int i in numbers)

{

Console.Write(" " + i);

}

Console.WriteLine();
```

```
string[] towns = { "London", "Paris",
"Milan", "New York" };

foreach (string town in towns)

{

Console.Write(" " + town);

}
```

In the example above, we created an array and then printed those numbers on the output screen using a foreach loop. Similarly, an array of strings is created and printed onto the output window.

Nested Loops

As the name suggests, a nested loop has multiple loops within the main loop. The syntax is as follows:

```
for (initialization, verification, update)

{

for (initialization, verification, update)

{

        Body;

}

}
```

If the condition holds true in the main loop, the statements within the main loop are executed. Before you write a code with nested loops, it is important to write down the algorithm. You should determine how you want to organize the loops. Let's assume you want to print the numbers in the following format:

```
1

1 2

1 2 3

1 2 3 ...... n
```

You need two loops – the outer loop to look at the number of lines being executed and the inner loop to look at the elements within each line. The code has been given in the last chapter.

Continue Statement

The continue statement makes the loop skip the rest of the loop body and test the condition before iterating over the sequence. The following example describes the function of the statement.

```
int n = int.Parse(Console.ReadLine());

int sum = 0;

for (int i = 1; i <= n; i += 2)

{

if (i % 8 == 0)

{

continue;

}
```

```
    sum += i;

}

Console.WriteLine("sum = " + sum);
```

In the above program, we calculate the sum of the integers not divisible by 8. The loop will run until it reaches a number that cannot be divided by 8.

Chapter Eleven

Mistakes to Avoid Making
While Coding in an Interview

People who never make mistakes are people who have never done anything at all. This section covers some of the most common mistakes made and how you can avoid making those mistakes.

Using Incorrect Cases for Letters

You will be making a blunder if you put capital letters where they do not belong when writing a program in any programming language. Track every alphabet you will be using when writing a program. Here are a few things to keep in mind when you are writing your code:

Every keyword in some programming languages is lowercase. For instance, when you are using the keyword "public," you cannot write it as "Public" or "PUBLIC."

If you are using names from the programming language's API, ensure the names match what appears in the API.

Capitalize and spell every variable the same way across the program. If you have declared a variable called "Myhouse," you cannot refer to it as "myhouse" or "MYHOUSE." If you use the same variable in multiple ways, the programming language will assume you have different and distinct variables with the same name.

Break Out of a Switch Statement

If you forget to break out of a switch statement, your compiler will not go past the Switch statement. For example,

```
switch (verse)

{

case 3:
```

```
printf("Please remember, ");

printf("please remember,");

case 2:

printf("I am in pain, ");

printf("i am in pain,");

case 1:

printf("I need  medicine, ");

printf("i need medicine,");

}
```

If there is no break at the end of each case, the computer will print the first sentence from each case. The code should therefore be,

```
switch (verse)

{

case 3:

printf("Please remember, ");

printf("please remember,");

break

case 2:

printf("I am in pain, ");

printf("i am in pain,");
```

```
break

case 1:

printf("I need  medicine, ");

printf("i need medicine,");

break

}
```

Using Double Equal signs

You have to use double equal signs in any programming language. If you were to use single equal signs, you would find the code does not provide the desired results. For example, if you were to write,

```
If (X=Y)
```

you are saying the value of Y should be given to the value of X.

However, if you were to use the following code:

```
If (X == Y)
```

you are asking the compiler to verify if the X and Y values are the same.

Adding components to the interface

Here is an example of a constructor you can use in a frame:

```
public SimpleFrame()

{
```

```
JButton button = new JButton("Thank
you...");

setTitle("...Connie Santisteban and Brian
Walls");

setLayout(new FlowLayout());

add(button);

button.addActionListener(this);

setSize(300, 100);

setVisible(true);

}
```

No matter what you do, you should add the "add" method. If you do not use this method, all your effort to add a button to your frame goes to waste.

Adding Listeners

Using the same example as above, if you forget to add the addActionListener method, you will find the button does not perform the function you want it to.

Defining the Constructors

When you define a constructor using parameters, your compiler will never accept it if you define the constructor without the parameter. For example, if you were to define a constructor in the following way: public Temperature (double number), you cannot call the function Temperature without a parameter.

Fixing References

Consider the following code:

```
class WillNotWork

{

String greeting = "Hello";

    public static void main(String args[])

{

Printf(greeting);

}

}
```

When you type this code in any programming language and run it, you will obtain an error since the method "main" is static, but the method "greeting" is not static.

Staying within an Array's Bounds

When you declare an array with ten different components, each component will have indices between 0 and 9. This has been explained in the previous chapters. If you declare the following:

```
int students[] = new int[10];
```

You can refer to the "students" array's components by writing students[0], students[1], all the way up to students[9]. You cannot use the students[10] since there is no component in the array with an index of 10.

Anticipating Null Pointers

Most of the examples used in this book do not give the NullPointerException error, but when you are writing new codes in any programming language, you will see this exception most of the time. This exception occurs only when you use methods with no return value. Consider the following example:

```
# include <stdio.h>

class ListMyFiles

{

    public static void main(String args[])

    {

        File myFile = new File("\\windows");

    String dir[] = myFile.list();

        for (String fileName : dir)

    {

    printf(fileName);

    }

    }

    }
```

This program will display the list of files present in the windows directory. What happens when you change \\windows to something else? What if you were to use a variable dissociated from a directory?

```
File myFile = new File("&*%$!!");
```

The new File call will return a null, meaning there will be nothing the function can return. This means there will be nothing in the "myFile" variable. The variable "dir," later in the code, refers to absolutely nothing, and the attempt to use a loop using the "dir" fails. You get a big NullPointerException, and the program comes crashing down around you.

To avoid this kind of error, you should go through the language's API Documentation. Add an exception handling code to the program if you want to use a function returning a null value.

Helping the Processor Find Files

You are working on your code, minding your own business when your computer throws the following error at you – "NoClassDefFoundError." A lot of things could be going wrong, but there are chances your computer could not find a file in particular. To fix this, you will have to align your code accurately:

- The project directory will contain the names of all files being used in your code.

- If you have used packages in your code, your project directory will have subdirectories with appropriate names.

- The CLASSPATH will be set properly.

Chapter Twelve

Example Programs to
Review before the Interview

Search Algorithms

The following points must be kept in mind when writing an algorithm during the interview. The interviewer may ask you to write down an algorithm, so he can understand how you think about a certain problem.

- You have to sort the elements in the array before you use the algorithm

- The optimal length the compiler must traverse through is $\sqrt{n}$. Therefore, the time complexity of this algorithm is $O(\sqrt{n})$. This indicates the binary search and linear search algorithms are performed together to ensure the algorithm is not too complex

- The jump search algorithm is not as good as the binary search algorithm in terms of efficiency, but it is better than the binary search algorithm since the compiler only moves once through the array. If the binary search algorithm is too expensive in terms of memory and time, use the jump search algorithm instead

Linear Search

Using the example below, we will understand how a linear search can be performed on an array. In the problem, we will consider an array and use a function to find the element in the array. Since the linear search algorithm checks every element in the array, it will traverse through the entire data structure. It is for this reason this search algorithm is not efficient.

For instance, if you want to look for the element 16 in an array, the algorithm will go through each element to look for the number.

```
Aray1[] = {1, 4, 16, 5, 19, 10}
```

Output:

```
16
```

It will also return the index of the number.

Let us assume the number is not present in the array; what do you think will happen then? Let us look for the number 45.

Output: -1

To perform a linear search algorithm, use the steps given below:

- Define the array and add numbers to it

- Identify the element you want to search for

- Begin with the leftmost element present in the array

- Compare the target element with each of the elements in the array

- If the target element matches the element in the array, return the index

- If the target element is not present, return -1

Implementation

```
#include <stdio.h>

int search(int arr[], int n, int x)

{

    int i;

    for (i = 0; i < n; i++)
```

```
            if (arr[i] == x)

                return i;

        return -1;

    }


int main(void)

    {

        int arr[] = { 2, 3, 4, 10, 40 };

        int x = 10;

        int n = sizeof(arr) / sizeof(arr[0]);

        int result = search(arr, n, x);

        (result == -1) ? printf("Element is not
    present in array")

                     : printf("Element is
    present at index %d",

                            result);

        return 0;

    }
```

Binary Search

The binary search algorithm does not work well with unsorted information. This means you should first use the sorting algorithm to clean up the data and store the information in an array. You should then write a function to find the element in the array you are looking for. A binary search algorithm breaks the array into segments and performs a linear search on the segment to find the required element. It is easier to perform a linear search, but a binary search is more efficient.

This algorithm will ignore the other elements in the array after it performs one comparison. Follow the steps given below to perform a binary search on the array elements:

1. Define the array and list the elements in the array. List the element you want to search for

2. Sort the elements in the array. Now, compare the target element with the middle element

3. If the element is the same, return the index or location of the element

4. If the target element is greater than the middle element, it will be present in the section to the right of the middle element. If it is lesser than the middle element, it will be present in the section to the left of the middle element

5. Perform the steps from 2 – 4 with the left or right section of the array

6. Otherwise, check the other half

7. End the search

Implementation

```c
#include <stdio.h>

// This program is an example of a recursive
binary search function. It will return the
location of x in the given array arr[l..r]
if the element is present. Otherwise, it
returns the value -1

int binarySearch(int arr[], int l, int r,
int x)

{

    if (r >= l) {

        int mid = l + (r - l) / 2;

        // If the element is the same as the
element in the middle of the array, then it
returns the index of the middle element

        if (arr[mid] == x)

        return mid;



        // If an element is smaller than the
middle element, then the element will only
be present in the left section of the array.
We will now perform a search on the section

        if (arr[mid] > x)

        return binarySearch(arr, l, mid
- 1, x);
```

```c
        // Else, the element can only be
present in the right section of the array

        return binarySearch(arr, mid + 1, r,
x);

    }



    // We reach here when the element is not
present in the array itself

    return -1;

}

int main(void)

{

    int arr[] = { 2, 3, 4, 10, 40 };

    int n = sizeof(arr) / sizeof(arr[0]);

    int x = 10;

    int result = binarySearch(arr, 0, n - 1,
x);

    (result == -1) ? printf("Element is not
present in array")

                   : printf("Element is
present at index %d",

                        result);
```

```
            return 0;

        }
```

In the next step we will look at how you can implement the algorithm using both the recursive and iterative methods. Before this, it is important to understand the time complexity of any binary search algorithm, especially to ensure you do not spend the machine's time unnecessarily on compiling. The formula to use is: $T(n) = T(n/2) + c$. To remove the recurrence in the code, use a recurrence or master tree method.

Recursive implementation

```cpp
// To implement recursive Binary Search
using C++

#include <bits/stdc++.h>

using namespace std;



// In this code, we will use a recursive
binary search function. It returns the
location of the variable x in a given array
arr[1..r] is present.

// otherwise it will return the value -1

int binarySearch(int arr[], int l, int r,
int x)

{

    if (r >= l) {
```

```
        int mid = l + (r - l) / 2;



        // If the element is present in the
middle of the array

        if (arr[mid] == x)

            return mid;



        // If the element is smaller than
mid, then it indicates the element is
present in the left subarray

        if (arr[mid] > x)

            return binarySearch(arr, l, mid
- 1, x);



        // Else, the element can only be
present in the other section of the array

            return binarySearch(arr, mid + 1, r,
x);

    }



    // If the element is not present in the
array, the compiler reaches this point

    return -1;
```

```
}


int main(void)

{

    int arr[] = { 2, 3, 4, 10, 40 };

    int x = 10;

    int n = sizeof(arr) / sizeof(arr[0]);

    int result = binarySearch(arr, 0, n - 1,
x);

    (result == -1) ? cout << "Element is not
present in array"

                    : cout << "Element is
present at index " << result;

    return 0;

}
```

The output of the code is:

```
        Element is present at index 3
```

Iterative implementation

```
// To implement recursive Binary Search
using C++

#include <bits/stdc++.h>

using namespace std;
```

```
// In this code, we will use a recursive
binary search function. It returns the
location of the variable x in a given array
arr[l..r] is present.

// otherwise, it will return the value -1

int binarySearch(int arr[], int l, int r,
int x)

{

    while (l <= r) {

        int m = l + (r - l) / 2;


        // Check if x is present at mid

        if (arr[m] == x)

            return m;


        // If x is greater, ignore the left
half of the array

        if (arr[m] < x)

            l = m + 1;


        // If x is smaller, ignore right
half of the array
```

```
        else

            r = m - 1;

    }



    // If the compiler does not find the
element in the array, the compiler reaches
this stage

    return -1;

}



int main(void)

{

    int arr[] = { 2, 3, 4, 10, 40 };

    int x = 10;

    int n = sizeof(arr) / sizeof(arr[0]);

    int result = binarySearch(arr, 0, n - 1,
x);

    (result == -1) ? cout << "Element is not
present in array"

                : cout << "Element is
present at index " << result;

    return 0;
```

```
}
```

The output of the code is:

```
Element is present at index 3
```

Jump Search

This algorithm is like the binary search algorithm. It looks for the element you want to find in the array. Bear in mind, like the binary search algorithm, that the jump search algorithm only works if the array is sorted. This algorithm aims to look for the element from a smaller section of the array. This means the compiler skips some elements in the array to jump to another section in the algorithm.

Let us look at an example to understand this concept better. Let's assume you have created an array with 'n' elements in them. You can indicate to the compiler to jump ahead by a few steps. If you want to look for the search element in the array, you begin to look at the following indices a[0], a[m], a[2m], ….. a[km]. The linear search will begin if the compiler finds the interval where the element may be present.

Consider the following array: (0, 1, 1, 2, 3, 5, 8, 13, 21, 34, 55, 89, 144, 233, 377, 610). There are 16 elements in this array. Now, let us indicate to the compiler to look for 55 in the array, and we will tell the compiler to break the code down into four subsections. This indicates the compiler will move by four elements every time.

Step 1: The compiler moves from the index 0 to 2.

Step 2: The compiler moves from 3 to 13.

Step 3: The compiler jumps from 21 to 89.

Step 4: The element in position 12 is larger than 55, so we go back to the start of the block.

Step 5: The linear search algorithm kicks in and looks for the index of the element.

Optimal Block Size

If you use the jump search algorithm, choose the right block size so that the compiler does not come across too many issues in the algorithm. In some cases, you may traverse through the entire list, but this depends on where the element is and how well you optimize the code. Sometimes, you have to perform m-1 comparisons when the linear search algorithm kicks in. This is the worst-case scenario, and it means the number of jumps will be ((n/m) + m-1). The value of this function will be minimum if the value of the element 'm' is square root n. Therefore, m = $\sqrt{n}$ is the number of steps the compiler has to run.

```
// To implement Jump Search using C++

    #include <bits/stdc++.h>

using namespace std;


int jumpSearch(int arr[], int x, int n)

{

    // Finding block size to be jumped
```

```
int step = sqrt(n);


// Finding the block where the element
is

// present (if it is present)

int prev = 0;

while (arr[min(step, n)-1] < x)

{

    prev = step;

    step += sqrt(n);

    if (prev >= n)

        return -1;

}


// Doing a linear search for x in block

// beginning with prev.

while (arr[prev] < x)

{

    prev++;
```

```
        // If we reached the next block or
end of

        // array, the element is not
present.

        if (prev == min(step, n))

            return -1;

    }

    // If the element is found

    if (arr[prev] == x)

        return prev;


    return -1;

}


// Driver program to test function

int main()

{

    int arr[] = { 0, 1, 1, 2, 3, 5, 8, 13,
21,

                  34, 55, 89, 144, 233, 377,
610 };

    int x = 55;
```

```
int n = sizeof(arr) / sizeof(arr[0]);


// Find the index of 'x' using Jump
Search

int index = jumpSearch(arr, x, n);


// Print the index where 'x' is located

count << "\nNumber " << x << " is at
index " << index;

return 0;

}
```

The output of this code:

```
Number 55 is at index 10
```

Sorting Algorithms

Quick Sort

This algorithm uses the concept of the divide and conquer algorithm. It picks the elements in an array and divides them into segments. It then chooses an element from the array as a pivot and splits the array into segments based on the pivot. You can perform a quick sort using one of the following methods:

1. Choose the median of the elements as the pivot

2. Choose the last element in the array as the pivot

3. Choose any random element as the pivot

4. Choose the first element in the array as the pivot

The important part of this process is the partition or utility function. This function's objective is to sort the elements in an array based on a pivot. So, it will take the pivot, place the pivot in the middle and order the other elements.

```
Implementation

#include<stdio.h>

// We will now introduce a utility function
used to swap two elements in the array

void swap(int* a, int* b)

{

    int t = *a;

    *a = *b;

    *b = t;

}

/* This utility function uses the last
element as the pivot and places the pivot
element at its correct position in the
sorted array. The function then places all
smaller (smaller than pivot) to the left of
```

the pivot and all the larger elements in the array to the right of the pivot element */

```c
int partition (int arr[], int low, int high)

{

    int pivot = arr[high];    // pivot

    int i = (low - 1);   // Index of smaller element


    for (int j = low; j <= high- 1; j++)

    {

        // If the current element is smaller than the pivot

        if (arr[j] < pivot)

        {

            i++;    // increment index of smaller element

            swap(&arr[i], &arr[j]);

        }

    }

    swap(&arr[i + 1], &arr[high]);

    return (i + 1);

}
```

```
/* The main function implements QuickSort

 arr[] --> Array to be sorted,

  low  --> Starting index,

  high  --> Ending index */

void quickSort(int arr[], int low, int high)

{

    if (low < high)

    {

        /* pi is partitioning index, arr[p]
is now

        at the right place */

        int pi = partition(arr, low, high);


        // Separately sort elements before

        // partition and after partition

        quickSort(arr, low, pi - 1);

        quickSort(arr, pi + 1, high);

    }

}
```

```c
/* Function to print an array */
void printArray(int arr[], int size)
{
    int i;
    for (i=0; i < size; i++)
        printf("%d ", arr[i]);
    printf("n");
}


// Driver program to test the above functions
int main()
{
    int arr[] = {10, 7, 8, 9, 1, 5};
    int n = sizeof(arr)/sizeof(arr[0]);
    quickSort(arr, 0, n-1);
    printf("Sorted array: n");
    printArray(arr, n);
    return 0;
```

```
    }
```

Understanding the partition algorithm

```
/* low  --> Starting index,  high  -->
Ending index */

quickSort(arr[], low, high)

{

    if (low < high)

    {

        /* pi is partitioning index, arr[pi]
is now

        at the right place */

        pi = partition(arr, low, high);


        quickSort(arr, low, pi - 1);  //
Before pi

        quickSort(arr, pi + 1, high); //
After pi

    }

}
```

The pseudo-code for the partition algorithm is:

```
/* low  --> Starting index,  high  -->
Ending index */
```

```
quickSort(arr[], low, high)

{

    if (low < high)

    {

        /* pi is partitioning index, arr[pi]
is now

            at the right place */

        pi = partition(arr, low, high);


        quickSort(arr, low, pi - 1);  //
Before pi

        quickSort(arr, pi + 1, high); //
After pi

    }

}

/* This function takes the last element as a
pivot, places

    the pivot element at its correct position
in sorted

    array, and places all smaller (smaller
than pivot)

    to the left of the pivot and all greater
elements to the right
```

```
of pivot */

partition (arr[], low, high)

{

    // pivot (Element to be placed at right
position)

    pivot = arr[high];



    i = (low - 1)   // Index of smaller
element



    for (j = low; j <= high- 1; j++)

    {

        // If the current element is smaller
than the pivot

        if (arr[j] < pivot)

        {

            i++;     // increment index of
smaller element

            swap arr[i] and arr[j]

        }

    }

    swap arr[i + 1] and arr[high])
```

```
    return (i + 1)

}
```

Let us look at the illustration of this function:

```
arr[] = {10, 80, 30, 90, 40, 50, 70}

Indexes:  0   1   2   3   4   5   6
```

low = 0, high = 6, pivot = arr[h] = 70

Initialize index of smaller element, i = -1

Traverse elements from j = low to high-1

j = 0 : Since arr[j] <= pivot, do i++ and swap(arr[i], arr[j])

i = 0

```
arr[] = {10, 80, 30, 90, 40, 50, 70} // No
change as i and j
```

```
                                    // are
same
```

j = 1 : Since arr[j] > pivot, do nothing

// No change in i and arr[]

```
j = 2 : Since arr[j] <= pivot, do i++ and
swap(arr[i], arr[j])

i = 1

arr[] = {10, 30, 80, 90, 40, 50, 70} // We
swap 80 and 30



j = 3 : Since arr[j] > pivot, do nothing

// No change in i and arr[]



j = 4 : Since arr[j] <= pivot, do i++ and
swap(arr[i], arr[j])

i = 2

arr[] = {10, 30, 40, 90, 80, 50, 70} // 80
and 40 Swapped

j = 5 : Since arr[j] <= pivot, do i++ and
swap arr[i] with arr[j]

i = 3

arr[] = {10, 30, 40, 50, 80, 90, 70} // 90
and 50 Swapped
```

We come out of the loop because j is now equal to high-1.

Finally, we place the pivot at the correct position by swapping

```
arr[i+1] and arr[high] (or pivot)

arr[] = {10, 30, 40, 50, 70, 90, 80} // 80
and 70 Swapped
```

Now 70 is at its correct place. All elements smaller than 70 are before it, and all elements greater than 70 are after it.

Let us look at how to implement this algorithm in C++:

```cpp
/* C++ implementation of QuickSort */

#include <bits/stdc++.h>

using namespace std;


// A utility function to swap two elements

void swap(int* a, int* b)

{

    int t = *a;

    *a = *b;

    *b = t;

}


/* This function takes the last element as a
pivot, places
```

the pivot element at its correct position in sorted

array, and places all smaller (smaller than pivot)

to the left of the pivot and all greater elements to the right

of pivot */

```c
int partition (int arr[], int low, int high)

{

    int pivot = arr[high]; // pivot

    int i = (low - 1); // Index of smaller element


    for (int j = low; j <= high - 1; j++)

    {

        // If the current element is smaller than the pivot

        if (arr[j] < pivot)

        {

            i++; // increment index of smaller element

            swap(&arr[i], &arr[j]);

        }
```

```
    }

    swap(&arr[i + 1], &arr[high]);

    return (i + 1);

}


/* The main function implements QuickSort

arr[] --> Array to be sorted,

low --> Starting index,

high --> Ending index */

void quickSort(int arr[], int low, int high)

{

    if (low < high)

    {

        /* pi is partitioning index, arr[p]
is now

        at the right place */

        int pi = partition(arr, low, high);


        // Separately sort elements before

        // partition and after partition
```

```cpp
        quickSort(arr, low, pi - 1);

        quickSort(arr, pi + 1, high);

    }

}


/* Function to print an array */

void printArray(int arr[], int size)

{

    int i;

    for (i = 0; i < size; i++)

        cout << arr[i] << " ";

    cout << endl;

}


// Driver Code

int main()

{

    int arr[] = {10, 7, 8, 9, 1, 5};

    int n = sizeof(arr) / sizeof(arr[0]);

    quickSort(arr, 0, n - 1);
```

```
cout << "Sorted array: \n";

printArray(arr, n);

return 0;
```

}

Selection Sort

The selection sort algorithm breaks the array into segments and sorts each segment by looking for the minimum element in the unsorted segment and moving it to the front of the array. The algorithm maintains two segments:

1. The sorted segment

2. The remaining part of the array that the algorithm should sort

In each iteration, the algorithm moves the minimum element from the unsorted segment to the sorted segment.

Let us consider the following example:

We have an array array1[] = {10, 65, 40, 12, 22}. The objective is to find the minimum element in the above array and move it to the beginning of the array. Since the minimum element is at the start of the array, the array will not change.

```
array1[] = {10, 65, 40, 12, 22}
```

Now, the algorithm will look for the minimum element between the second and last element and move it to the smaller one to the beginning. The array will now look as follows:

```
array1[] = {10, 12, 65, 40, 22}
```

The algorithm will continue to break the array into segments, and the output will be:

```
array1[] = {10, 12, 22, 40, 65}
```

Implementation

```c
#include<stdio.h>

int main(){

    /* Using this program, the variables i
    and j are loop counters. The variable temp
    is used for swapping, and it holds the total
    number of elements in the array.

    * The variable number[] is used to store
    all the input elements for the array, and
    the size of this array will change based on
    necessity. */

    int i, j, count, temp, number[25];

    printf("Number of elements: ");

    scanf("%d",&count);

    printf("Enter %d elements: ", count);

    // Loop to get the elements stored in the
    array
```

```
for(i=0;i<count;i++)

    scanf("%d",&number[i]);

// Logic of selection sort algorithm

for(i=0;i<count;i++){

    for(j=i+1;j<count;j++){

        if(number[i]>number[j]){

            temp=number[i];

            number[i]=number[j];

            number[j]=temp;

        }

    }

}

printf("Sorted elements: ");

for(i=0;i<count;i++)

    printf(" %d",number[i]);

return 0;

}
```

Bubble Sort

The bubble sort algorithm is a very simple and easy-to-use sorting algorithm. It compares adjacent elements and sorts the elements based on the ascending order. If the position of the elements does not change, the elements are sorted. The process followed using this sorting algorithm is stated below:

1. Define the array and its elements

2. Use a statement to calculate the length of the array and store the number in the variable 'n'

3. The following steps should be performed for the elements in the array:

4. Using the loop covering the elements starting with the index (i) = 1 and ending at n and another loop for every element starting with index (j) = n and ending at i+1, perform the following steps:

    a. If A[j] < A[j-1]

    b. Move the element at the index Array [j] to the position Array [j-1]

5. End the algorithm

Consider the following example:

First Pass:

        (5 1 4 2 8) -> (1 5 4 2 8):

In this step, the algorithm will compare the elements in the array and swap the numbers 1 and 5.

        (1 5 4 2 8) ->   (1 4 5 2 8):

In this step, the numbers 4 and 5 are swapped since the number 5 is greater than 4.

```
( 1 4 5 2 8 ) -> ( 1 4 2 5 8 ):
```

In this step, the numbers 5 and 2 are swapped.

```
( 1 4 2 5 8 ) -> ( 1 4 2 5 8 ):
```

In the last step, the elements are ordered, so no more swapping is necessary.

Second Pass:

```
( 1 4 2 5 8 ) -> ( 1 4 2 5 8 )
```

```
( 1 4 2 5 8 ) -> ( 1 2 4 5 8 ):
```

In this step, the numbers 4 and 2 are swapped since the number 4 is greater than 2.

```
( 1 2 4 5 8 ) -> ( 1 2 4 5 8 )
```

```
( 1 2 4 5 8 ) -> ( 1 2 4 5 8 )
```

Since the compiler cannot determine whether the array is sorted, it will run the code again.

Third Pass:

```
( 1 2 4 5 8 ) -> ( 1 2 4 5 8 )
```

```
( 1 2 4 5 8 ) -> ( 1 2 4 5 8 )
```

```
( 1 2 4 5 8 ) -> ( 1 2 4 5 8 )
```

```
( 1 2 4 5 8 ) -> ( 1 2 4 5 8 )
```

Consider the following implementations of the bubble sort algorithm:

```cpp
// Implementation of the algorithm in C++

#include <bits/stdc++.h>

using namespace std;


void swap(int *xp, int *yp)

{

    int temp = *xp;

    *xp = *yp;

    *yp = temp;

}


// A function to implement bubble sort

void bubbleSort(int arr[], int n)

{

    int i, j;

    for (i = 0; i < n-1; i++)
```

```cpp
    // Last i elements are already in place

    for (j = 0; j < n-i-1; j++)

        if (arr[j] > arr[j+1])

            swap(&arr[j], &arr[j+1]);
}


/* Function to print an array */
void printArray(int arr[], int size)
{
    int i;
    for (i = 0; i < size; i++)
        cout << arr[i] << " ";
    cout << endl;
}


// Driver code
int main()
{
    int arr[] = {64, 34, 25, 12, 22, 11, 90};
```

```
    int n = sizeof(arr)/sizeof(arr[0]);

    bubbleSort(arr, n);

    cout<<"Sorted array: \n";

    printArray(arr, n);

    return 0;

}
```

The output of this code is:

Sorted array:

```
11 12 22 25 34 64 90
```

Insertion Sort

The insertion sort algorithm is very simple to use. The algorithm works the same way as the process you use to sort playing cards. The algorithm follows the process below:

1. Create an array with any number of elements, and define it using the following method: array1 [n]

2. Use a loop function and run it from the first element in the array until the end of the array. Now, choose the element and insert the element into the sequence

3. Add a condition so the element is included in the array based on its array size

4. End the algorithm

Let us consider the following example:

Define an array Array1[5] and add variables to the array: Array1[] = {12, 11, 13, 5, 6}. Now, add a loop to the array and begin the function from the first element. The loop should move until the last element in the array. Since the second number is less than the first number, the algorithm will move it before 11.

```
Array1[] = {11, 12, 13, 5, 6}
```

The loop now moves to the third element in the array, but the array will change since the elements before the third element are smaller than the third element.

```
Array1[] = {11, 12, 13, 5, 6}
```

Now, the loop moves to the fourth element in the array and compares the other elements in the array with the previous numbers in the array. Since the number is smaller than all the other numbers, it will move to the front.

```
Array1[] = {5, 11, 12, 13, 6}
```

The loop finally moves to the last number in the array, and since this number is less than the three numbers before it but greater than the first number, it will move to the second position.

```
Array1[] = {5, 6, 11, 12, 13}

Implementation

#include <math.h>
```

```c
#include <stdio.h>

/* Function to sort an array using
insertion sort*/

void insertionSort(int arr[], int n)

{

    int i, key, j;

    for (i = 1; i < n; i++) {

        key = arr[i];

        j = i - 1;

        /* Move elements of arr[0..i-1]

        greater than key, to one position
ahead

        of their current position */

        while (j >= 0 && arr[j] > key) {

            arr[j + 1] = arr[j];

            j = j - 1;

        }

        arr[j + 1] = key;

    }

}
```

```c
// A utility function to print an array of
size n

void printArray(int arr[], int n)

{

    int i;

    for (i = 0; i < n; i++)

        printf("%d ", arr[i]);

    printf("\n");

}

/* Driver program to test insertion sort
*/

int main()

{

    int arr[] = { 12, 11, 13, 5, 6 };

    int n = sizeof(arr) / sizeof(arr[0]);

        insertionSort(arr, n);

    printArray(arr, n);

        return 0;

}
```

Merge Sort

Like the quick sort algorithm, the merge sort algorithm works like a divide and conquer algorithm. In this sorting algorithm, the input array is broken into two halves. The sorting algorithm will be called to sort the elements in each of the halves and then merge the array into one array. You can use the merge function to merge the two halves. You have to enter the following parameters when you perform a merge sort algorithm:

1. The input array, along with its elements

2. First sorted half

3. Second sorted half

Using the merge sort algorithm, you can merge the two arrays. Let's first look at how the algorithm functions before we look at the implementation.

1. Define the array and add the elements to it

2. Divide the array into halves, and sort the elements in each half

3. Use the merge function to combine the sorted arrays

4. End the algorithm

Implementation

// Using this code, we will merge two subarrays of the array arr[]. The first subarray is arr[l..m] and the second is arr[m+1..r]

```c
void merge(int arr[], int l, int m, int r)

{

    int i, j, k;

    int n1 = m - l + 1;

    int n2 =  r - m;


    /* create temp arrays */

    int L[n1], R[n2];


    /* Copy data to temp arrays L[] and R[]
*/

    for (i = 0; i < n1; i++)

        L[i] = arr[l + i];

    for (j = 0; j < n2; j++)

        R[j] = arr[m + 1+ j];


    /* Merge the temp arrays back into
arr[l..r]*/

    i = 0; // Initial index of first
subarray

    j = 0; // Initial index of second
subarray
```

```
k = 1; // Initial index of merged
subarray

while (i < n1 && j < n2)

{

    if (L[i] <= R[j])

    {

        arr[k] = L[i];

        i++;

    }

    else

    {

        arr[k] = R[j];

        j++;

    }

    k++;

}


/* Copy the remaining elements of L[],
if there

    are any */

while (i < n1)
```

```
    {

        arr[k] = L[i];

        i++;

        k++;

    }


    /* Copy the remaining elements of R[],
if there

        are any */

    while (j < n2)

    {

        arr[k] = R[j];

        j++;

        k++;

    }

}


/* l is for the left index, and r is the
right index of the

    sub-array of arr to be sorted */

void mergeSort(int arr[], int l, int r)
```

```
{

    if (l < r)

    {

        // Same as (l+r)/2, but avoids
overflow for

        // large l and h

        int m = l+(r-l)/2;


        // Sort first and second halves

        mergeSort(arr, l, m);

        mergeSort(arr, m+1, r);


        merge(arr, l, m, r);

    }

}


/* UTILITY FUNCTIONS */

/* Function to print an array */

void printArray(int A[], int size)

{
```

```c
    int i;

    for (i=0; i < size; i++)

        printf("%d ", A[i]);

    printf("\n");

}


/* Driver program to test above functions */

int main()

{

    int arr[] = {12, 11, 13, 5, 6, 7};

    int arr_size =
sizeof(arr)/sizeof(arr[0]);


    printf("Given array is \n");

    printArray(arr, arr_size);


    mergeSort(arr, 0, arr_size - 1);


    printf("\nSorted array is \n");

    printArray(arr, arr_size);
```

```
            return 0;

    }
```

Important Concepts

Enhanced For Loop

```
    public class EnhancedFor

    {

        public static void main(String[] args)

        {    int[] list ={1, 2, 3, 4, 5, 6, 7,
8, 9, 10};

            int sum = sumListEnhanced(list);

            System.out.println("Sum of
elements in list: " + sum);



            System.out.println("Original
List");

            printList(list);

            System.out.println("Calling
addOne");

            addOne(list);

            System.out.println("List after
call to addOne");

            printList(list);
```

```
            System.out.println("Calling
addOneError");

            addOneError(list);

            System.out.println("List after a
call to addOneError. Note elements of the
list did not change.");

            printList(list);

      }



      // pre: list != null

      // post: return sum of elements

      // uses enhanced for loop

      public static int
sumListEnhanced(int[] list)

      {      int total = 0;

            for(int val : list)

            {      total += val;

            }

            return total;

      }



      // pre: list != null
```

```java
// post: return sum of elements

// use traditional for loop

public static int sumListOld(int[] list)

{       int total = 0;

        for(int i = 0; i < list.length; i++)

            {    total += list[i];

                 System.out.println( list[i] );

            }

        return total;

}


// pre: list != null

// post: none.

// The code appears to add one to every element in the list but does not

public static void addOneError(int[] list)

{       for(int val : list)

            {    val = val + 1;
```

```
        }

    }


    // pre: list != null

    // post: adds one to every element of
list

    public static void addOne(int[] list)

    {    for(int i = 0; i < list.length;
i++)

        {    list[i]++;

        }

    }

    public static void printList(int[]
list)

    {    System.out.println("index,
value");

        for(int i = 0; i < list.length;
i++)

        {    System.out.println(i + ", "
+ list[i]);

        }

    }

}
```

Recursion

```
public class RecursionExampleDirectory

{

    public int getSize(Directory dir)

    {    int total = 0;



        //check files

        File[] files = dir.getFiles();

        for(int i = 0; i < files.length;
i++)

            total +=
files[i].getSize();



        //get subdirectories and check
them

        Directory[] subs = dir.getSubs();

        for(int i = 0; i < subs.length;
i++)

            total += getSize(subs[i]);



        return total;

    }
```

```
public static void main(String[] args)

{      RecursionExampleDirectory r = new
RecursionExampleDirectory();

       Directory d = new Directory();

       System.out.println( r.getSize(d)
);

    }


//pre: n >= 0

public static int fact(int n)

{      int result = 0;

       if(n == 0)

            result = 1;

       else

            result = n * fact(n-1);

       return result;

    }


//pre: exp >= 0
```

```java
public static int pow(int base, int exp)
{       int result = 0;
        if(exp == 0)
                result = 1;
        else
                result = base * pow(base, exp - 1);
        return result;
}


//slow fib
//pre: n >= 1
public static int fib(int n)
{       int result = 0;
        if(n == 1 || n == 2)
                result = 1;
        else
                result = fib(n-1) + fib(n-2);
        return result;
```

```java
        }


    public static int minWasted(int[]
items, int itemNum, int capLeft)

    {      int result = 0;

        if(itemNum >= items.length)

            result = capLeft;

        else if( capLeft == 0)

            result = 0;

        else

        {      int minWithout =
minWasted(items, itemNum + 1, capLeft);

            if( capLeft <=
items[itemNum])

            {      int minWith =
minWasted(items, itemNum + 1, capLeft -
items[itemNum]);

                result =
Math.min(minWith, minWithout);

            }

            else

                result = minWithout;

        }
```

```
            return result;

    }

}


class Directory

{       private Directory[] mySubs;

        private File[] myFiles;


        public Directory()

        {       int numSubs = (int)(Math.random()
* 3);

                mySubs = new Directory[numSubs];

                int numFiles =
(int)(Math.random() * 10);

                myFiles = new File[numFiles];



                for(int i = 0; i <
myFiles.length; i++)

                        myFiles[i] = new File(
(int)(Math.random() * 1000 ) );

                for(int i = 0; i < mySubs.length;
i++)
```

```
            mySubs[i] = new
Directory();

    }


    public Directory[] getSubs()

    {      return mySubs;

    }


    public File[] getFiles()

    {      return myFiles;

    }

}


class File

{      private int iMySize;


    public File(int size)

    {      iMySize = size;

    }
```

```
    public int getSize()

    {      return iMySize;

    }

}
```

Creating a 2D Array

```
// 2d array manipulation examples

//import

import java.awt.Color;

public class FilterExample

{

    /*

        *pre: image != null, image.length >
1, image[0].length > 1

        *    image is a rectangular matrix,
neighborhoodSize > 0

        *post: return a smoothed version of
the image

        */

    public Color[][] smooth(Color[][]
image, int neighborhoodSize)

        {      //check precondition
```

```
        assert image != null &&
image.length > 1 && image[0].length > 1

                    && ( neighborhoodSize
> 0 ) && rectangularMatrix( image )

                    : "Violation of
precondition: smooth";



        Color[][] result = new
Color[image.length][image[0].length];



        for(int row = 0; row <
image.length; row++)

        {    for(int col = 0; col <
image[0].length; col++)

            {    result[row][col] =
aveOfNeighbors(image, row, col,
neighborhoodSize);

            }

        }



        return result;

    }
```

```
// helper method determining the
average color of a neighborhood

// around a particular cell.

    private Color aveOfNeighbors(Color[][]
image, int row, int col, int
neighborhoodSize)

    {       int numNeighbors = 0;

            int red = 0;

            int green = 0;

            int blue = 0;


            for(int r = row -
neighborhoodSize; r <= row +
neighborhoodSize; r++)

            {      for(int c = col -
neighborhoodSize; c <= col +
neighborhoodSize; c++)

                {      if( inBounds( image,
r, c ) )

                    {      numNeighbors++;

                    red +=
image[r][c].getRed();

                    green +=
image[r][c].getGreen();
```

```
                                    blue +=
image[r][c].getBlue();

                        }

            }

    }


        assert numNeighbors > 0;

        return new Color( red /
numNeighbors, green / numNeighbors, blue /
numNeighbors );

    }



    //helper method to determine if given
coordinates are in bounds

    private boolean inBounds(Color[][]
image, int row, int col)

    {       return (row >= 0) && (row <=
image.length) && (col >= 0)

                    && (col <
image[0].length);

    }



    //private method to ensure the mat is
rectangular
```

```java
        private boolean rectangularMatrix(
Color[][] mat )

        {    boolean isRectangular = true;

            int row = 1;

            final int COLUMNS =
mat[0].length;


            while( isRectangular && row <
mat.length )

                {    isRectangular = (
mat[row].length == COLUMNS );

                    row++;

                }


            return isRectangular;

        }

    }
```

Creating Minesweeper

```java
    public class MineSweeper

    {    private int[][] myTruth;

        private boolean[][] myShow;
```

```java
    public void cellPicked(int row, int
col)

    {     if( inBounds(row, col) &&
!myShow[row][col] )

        {     myShow[row][col] = true;


            if( myTruth[row][col] == 0)

                {     for(int r = -1; r <=
1; r++)

                    for(int c = -1;
c <= 1; c++)

    cellPicked(row + r, col + c);

                    }

            }

        }


    public boolean inBounds(int row, int
col)

    {     return 0 <= row && row <
myTruth.length && 0 <= col && col <
myTruth[0].length;

        }

    }
```

Generating Lists

```java
import java.util.Collection;

import java.util.Iterator;


/**

 * A class to provide a simple list.

 * List resizes automatically. Used to
illustrate

 * various design and implementation details
of

 * a class in Java.

 *

 * @author scottm

 *

 */

public class GenericListVersion2 implements
Iterable{

    // class constant for default size

    private static final int DEFAULT_CAP =
10;


    //instance variables
```

```java
    // iValues store the elements of the
list and

    // may have extra capacity

    private Object[] iValues;

    private int iSize;



    private class GenericListIterator
implements Iterator{

        private int position;

        private boolean removeOK;



        private GenericListIterator(){

            position = 0;

            removeOK = false;

        }



        public boolean hasNext(){

            return position < iSize;

        }



        public Object next(){
```

```
             Object result =
iValues[position];

             position++;

             removeOK = true;

             return result;

        }


        public void remove(){

             if( !removeOK )

                 throw new
IllegalStateException();

             // which element should be
removed??

             removeOK = false;


GenericListVersion2.this.remove(position -
1);

             position--;

        }

    }


    public Iterator iterator(){
```

```
        return new GenericListIterator();

    }


    public void addAll(Collection c){

        // for each loop

        for(Object obj : c){

            this.add(obj);

        }

    }


    /**

     * Default add method. Add x to the end
of this IntList.

     * Size of the list goes up by 1.

     * @param x The value to add to the end
of this list.

     */

    public void add(Object x){

        insert(iSize, x);

    }
```

```java
public Object get(int pos){

    return iValues[pos];

}



/**

 * Insert obj at position pos.

 * post: get(pos) = x, size() = old
size() + 1

 * @param pos 0 <= pos <= size()

 * @param obj The element to add.

 */

public void insert(int pos, Object obj){

    ensureCapcity();

    for(int i = iSize; i > pos; i--){

        iValues[i] = iValues[i - 1];

    }

    iValues[pos] = obj;

    iSize++;

}
```

```
public Object remove(int pos){

    Object removedValue = iValues[pos];

    for(int i = pos; i < iSize - 1; i++)

        iValues[i] = iValues[i + 1];

    iValues[iSize - 1] = null;

    iSize--;

    return removedValue;

}


private void ensureCapcity(){

    // is there extra capacity
available?

    // if not, resize

    if(iSize == iValues.length)

        resize();

}


public int size(){

    return iSize;

}
```

```
    // resize internal storage container by
a factor of 2

    private void resize() {

        Object[] temp = new
Object[iValues.length * 2];

        System.arraycopy(iValues, 0, temp,
0, iValues.length);

        iValues = temp;

    }



    /**

    * Return a String version of this list.
Size and

    * elements included.

    */

    public String toString(){

        // we could make this more efficient
by using a StringBuffer.

        // See alternative version

        String result = "size: " + iSize +
", elements: [";

        for(int i = 0; i < iSize - 1; i++)
```

```
            result += iValues[i].toString()
+ ", ";

        if(iSize > 0 )

            result += iValues[iSize - 1];

        result += "]";

        return result;

    }



    // Would not really have this and
toString available

    // both included just for testing

    public String
toStringUsingStringBuffer(){

        StringBuffer result = new
StringBuffer();

        result.append( "size: " );

        result.append( iSize );

        result.append(", elements: [");

        for(int i = 0; i < iSize - 1; i++){

            result.append(iValues[i]);

            result.append(", ");

        }
```

```
        if( iSize > 0 )

            result.append(iValues[iSize -
1]);

        result.append("]");

        return result.toString();

    }


    /**

    * Default constructor. Creates an empty
list.

    */

    public GenericListVersion2(){

        //redirect to single int constructor

        this(DEFAULT_CAP);

        //other statements could go here.

    }


    /**

    * Constructor to allow the user of the
class to specify

    * initial capacity in case they intend
to add a lot
```

* of elements to the new list. Creates
an empty list.

    * @param initialCap > 0

    */

    public GenericListVersion2(int
initialCap) {

        assert initialCap > 0 : "Violation
of precondition. IntListVer1(int
initialCap):"

            + "initialCap should be greater
than 0. Value of initialCap: " + initialCap;

        iValues = new Object[initialCap];

        iSize = 0;

    }

    /**

    * Return true if this IntList is equal
to the other.

    * pre: none

    * @param other The object to compare to
this

    * @return true if other is a non-null,
IntList object

```
     * the same size as this IntList and has
the

     * same elements in the same order, false
otherwise.

     */

    public boolean equals(Object other){

         boolean result;

         if(other == null)

              // we know this is not null, so
it can't be equal

              result = false;

         else if(this == other)

              // quick check if this and other
refer to the same IntList object

              result = true;

         else if( this.getClass() !=
other.getClass() )

              // other is not an IntList they
can't be equal

              result = false;

         else{

              // other is not null and refers
to an IntList
```

```java
            GenericListVersion2 otherList =
(GenericListVersion2)other;

            result = this.size() ==
otherList.size();

            int i = 0;

            while(i < iSize && result){

            result =
this.iValues[i].equals( otherList.iValues[i]
);

                i++;

            }

        }

        return result;

    }

}
```

Linked List

```java
    package Fall0811;



    import java.util.Iterator;



    import Summer08.Node;
```

```java
public class LinkedList implements Iterable
{

    private Node head;

    private Node tail;

    private int size;


    public Iterator iterator(){

        return new LLIterator();

    }


    private class LLIterator implements
Iterator{

        private Node nextNode;

        private boolean removeOK;

        private int posToRemove;


        private LLIterator(){

            nextNode = head;

            removeOK = false;

            posToRemove = -1;

        }
```

```java
public boolean hasNext(){

    return nextNode != null;

}


public Object next(){

    assert hasNext();


    Object result =
nextNode.getData();

    nextNode = nextNode.getNext();


    removeOK = true;

    posToRemove++;


    return result;

}


public void remove(){

    assert removeOK;
```

```
            removeOK = false;


LinkedList.this.remove(posToRemove);

            posToRemove--;


        }

    }



    public void makeEmpty(){

        // let GC do its job!!!!!!!

        head = tail = null;

        size = 0;

    }



    public Object remove(int pos){

        assert pos >= 0 && pos < size;

        Object result;

        if( pos == 0 ){

            result = head.getData();

            head = head.getNext();

            if( size == 1 )
```

```
                    tail = null;

        }

        else{

            Node temp = head;

            for(int i = 1; i < pos; i++)

                temp = temp.getNext();

            result =
temp.getNext().getData();

            temp.setNext(
temp.getNext().getNext() );

            if( pos == size - 1)

                tail = temp;

        }

        size--;

        return result;

    }


    public Object get(int pos){

        assert pos >= 0 && pos < size;

        //array-based list

        // return myCon[pos]
```

```
Object result;

if( pos == size - 1 )

    result = tail.getData(); //O(1)

else{

    Node temp = head;

    for(int i = 0; i < pos; i++)

        temp = temp.getNext();

    result = temp.getData();

    // average case O(N) :((((

}

return result;

}


public void insert(int pos, Object obj){

    assert pos >= 0 && pos <= size;


    // addFirst?

    if(pos == 0)

        addFirst(obj); // O(1)

    // add last?
```

```
        else if( pos == size )

            add(obj); //at end O(1)

        else{

            // general case

            Node temp = head;

            for(int i = 1; i < pos; i++)

                temp = temp.getNext();

            // I know temp is pointing at
the

            // node at position pos - 1

            Node newNode = new Node(obj,
temp.getNext());

            temp.setNext( newNode );

            size++;

        }

    }


    public void add(Object obj){

        Node newNode = new Node(obj, null);

        if( size == 0 )

            head = newNode;
```

```
        else

            tail.setNext(newNode);

        tail = newNode;

        size++;

    }


    public void addFirst(Object obj){

        if(size == 0)

            add(obj);

        else{

            Node newNode = new Node(obj,
head);

            head = newNode;

            size++;

        }

    }


    public String toString(){

        String result = "";

        Node temp = head;
```

```
        for(int i = 0; i < size; i++){

            result += temp.getData() + " ";

            temp = temp.getNext();

        }

        return result;

    }

}
```

Conclusion

On that note, we have come to the end of this book. You now have a good idea about the coding interview and what skills you will have to work on before the interview begins. You also know what you should do after the interview. It is important to practice as often as you can so you appear confident in the interview. You will need a few hours to understand the important concepts. Therefore, you need to plan and study hard!

There is, unfortunately, no easy way out when it comes to a coding interview. You need to practice everything you study. You need to identify some behavioral questions the interviewer may ask you and prepare for them. Spend some time on the Internet and try to understand how the company assesses the candidates. You need to do this so you have a fair idea about how to prepare for the interview.

It is okay if you do not land this job. There is always something else out there for you. Learn from your interviews and improve so you do better in the next interview. Thank you for choosing this book. I wish you luck in your interviews.

Thank you for buying and reading/listening to our book. If you found this book useful/helpful please take a few minutes and leave a review on Amazon.com or Audible.com (if you bought the audio version).

Resources

Alexander, R. (2016, July 16). *Top 50 Programming Interview Questions & Answers ()*. Career.guru99.com.

Alex, R. (2017, June 22). *Top 50 Array Interview Questions & Answers (2022 Update)*. Career.guru99.com.

Coding interviews: Everything you need to prepare | Tech Interview Handbook. (2022, July 11).

Singh, V. (2022, July 6). *50+ Best Programming Interview Questions and Answers in 2022*. Hackr.io.

Sufiyan, T. (2020, December 22). *Top 40 Coding Interview Questions You Should Know*. Simplilearn.com.

Tay, Y. (2022, February 16). *How to Rock the Coding Interview – Tips That Helped Me Land Job Offers from Google, Airbnb, and Dropbox*. FreeCodeCamp.org

Technical Interviewing 101: Ultimate Guide to Acing Your Tech Interview in 2021. (2021, June 1). Learn to Code with Me.

The 24 Hours Before Your Interview | Interview Cake. (n.d.). Interview Cake: Programming Interview Questions and Tips.

Top 50 Array Coding Problems for Interviews. (2020, September 30). GeeksforGeeks.

What To Do After an Interview: 9 Tips to Help You Succeed. (2020, February 5). Indeed Career Guide.

www.ingramcontent.com/pod-product-compliance
Lightning Source LLC
Chambersburg PA
CBHW071423050326
40689CB00010B/1957